Drunk Toddlers and In-Laws:
Finding God in the Everyday

Megan Moody Collins

MEGAN MOODY COLLINS

Copyright © 2014 Megan Moody Collins

PREFACE
Coffee Shop Princess

3 p.m. is my kryptonite. It is the time of day when my energy runs low but there are still hours of life ahead. These are the hours when my children come home from school with their stories, when we scramble to make time for dinner together as a family, when my husband or I often rush back to church for an evening meeting, then when we steal a few minutes together to catch up as the darkness falls thick outside our window. 3 p.m. says I cannot possibly continue another moment, let alone another eight hours. Liar. That's why they make coffee.

One particular afternoon I passed through the doors of the coffee shop in our neighborhood, the promise of an alert afternoon wafting through the air with the heavy aroma of dark coffee. I am sure this is what heaven smells like. I stood with my fellow coffee drinkers, glazed and distracted, as we waited in line. A few moments later I retreated to a table in the corner, the warm paper cup clutched in my hand like a lifeline. I settled in to drink my beverage and take a moment of calm before beginning my day again, and took to watching the others around me.

Just next to my table I noticed a young mom, dressed in formal slacks and a blouse. Her shirt carried a few wrinkles from a long day at work, and her heels were crossed underneath the table. Across from her sat a blond little girl, who couldn't have been more than six. The mom held tight to her coffee cup as I did, but gave her undivided attention to the little girl who was chatting excitedly with the details of her day. A few moments later, the door to the shop opened again, and in walked a young man in the blue uniform of the local police department. His eyes met the woman's and they both smiled broadly, and he fell with a tired thump in to the seat next to her, greeting her with a kiss. I watched the sweet couple as they exchanged a few short words of affection. Their daughter bounced on the seat across from them, happy for the time with her parents.

As the mom rose to get another cup of coffee for her husband, the little girl grabbed her father's hand and pulled him to his feet. He followed her, with a curious smile, as she drug him in to the center of the coffee shop then stopped abruptly. "Daddy! You are the prince and I am the princess!" she said with certainty. She grabbed his large strong hands in her small ones, and began to twirl. Without hesitation, the father, in his full police uniform, began to sway back and forth. The coffee shop continued to buzz with conversation, but a few of us watched, transfixed, as the pair danced together, a young girl and her father. For that moment, time slowed down a bit. This was no longer just a coffee shop. This was a ball for a princess and her prince.

Our life is made of moments. Somedays moments blur together in to hours of seemingly insignificant events. We wonder what the purpose is of a day full of appointments. We struggle to find meaning in the mundane day to day. We can go through an entire week and not feel like anything of note has happened to us. Then there are times the moments grab our attention. The events stand out like snapshots in a photo album and we see God at work. We often remember these times as ones that changed us, whether through joy or even through suffering. These are the moments when we hear God's voice or we yell into the silence. We are surrounded by people or suffocated with loneliness. These are the peaks and valleys of our life, the highs and lows, that are countered by the longer stretches of flat ground.

We are only given a certain number of moments, and we want to make the most of them. We want to not miss the opportunities to care for the people in our lives, to grow in to the person God wants us to be, to be open to new directions and new adventures. We want to be like the people we read about in the Bible who follow God even when it means taking risks. We want to care more about what God thinks about us than what other people say.

We want to dance in coffee shops.

Even the most routine days offer the opportunity to challenge ourselves. Life happens to us as much when we are running a load of laundry or sitting in traffic as it does on exotic trips or in hospital rooms. God is there in every moment, not just the ones when we take notice. God is at work continually in our lives and in the world around us, with our without our awareness. The choices we make will influence not only the direction of our lives but how we experience the moments that make up our days. Each day, each minute, offers a choice.

> "Chose this day whom you will serve . . . as for me and my house
> we will serve the Lord." - Joshua 24:15 (NRSV)

Chapter 1
REALITY OVER PERFECTION
Drunk Toddlers and In-Laws

I have always been afraid of flying. Not appropriately afraid of flying, as many people are who feel a little shaky during take off. More in a hyperventilate when you print your boarding pass at home and then throw up half way down the tarmac kind of way. I know logically it doesn't make sense. I have read all of the statistics. I understand that it is mathematically proven to be much more safe to take an airplane than to drive in the car. I know there are safety measures in place, and back up safety measures in case those fail. But there is something about getting in that huge metal tube with wings and moving thousands of feet off the ground that makes my stomach flip. People often remind me before I fly that God will protect my family. While I do believe that God is there, I also am a little wary seeing as how there were exactly zero airplanes in the creation story. Perhaps God just meant for us to stay on the ground.

But despite my reservations, from time to time I do find myself on an airplane, hurtling through the air toward a destination deemed too far to travel in partnership with gravity via automobile. When my children were two and five, my husband's parents moved out to Oregon, which was exactly 2,520 miles from where we lived in Ohio. It came time for us to make a visit west to see them, and even I couldn't justify that amount of time in the car with two active young boys. The preparations began. I consider myself somewhat type A, and my typed packing list, which would already have reflected this tendency to obsess, had spiraled out of control. Instead of consciously worrying about the seven hours airborne, I channeled this concern in to making sure everything would be perfect when we landed to greet my in laws. I purchased new matching shirts for the boys. I packed extra toiletries in our carry on so we could freshen up before landing. I organized the boys' toys and snacks so they would be entertained and fed during the flight, therefore avoiding two children in meltdowns upon landing.

The night before our trip, everything was ready to go. Seeing as how I could not possibly repack our bags again, we decided a family trip to the pool was in order, to burn off energy (for the boys) and nervousness (for me). As I worked to get Elmo swimming trunks on to my squirmy toddler, his tiny hand moved upward more quickly than I anticipated, and I suddenly felt a searing pain in my right eye. I took a deep breath and waited for the pain to pass, but it didn't.

If anything, the pain seemed to intensify as I waited, and what had moments before been a working eye now only produced fuzzy shapes surrounded by painful halos of light. A quick one-eyed perusal of WedMd and I was off to the clinic. Three hours later I returned back home from the doctor, my eye full of drops to treat a scratched cornea. I was now also sporting a conspicuous black eye patch.

The next morning we walked down the corridor of the airport with the busy crowds of travelers jostling to get to their gates. My husband led the way, weighed down with suitcases, carry on bags, teddy bears, boarding passes and car seats. I followed behind him, complete with the black eye patch that I had been prescribed. My children, in their matching shirts, followed behind us, happily chanting "arrgh arrgh arrgh! She's a pirate!" to anyone who would listen. On we went through the airport halls attracting the stares of other harried travelers with our strange parade.

As we boarded the plane, I tried to think of ways I could potentially style my hair before landing to try and hide the patch. My vision of the perfect family disembarking the plane to greet my in-laws was not working out quite as I had hoped. Before we took off, the steward came around and greeted us, and he kindly only looked once at my eye patch before asking if we would like a drink. With this, my nervousness moved away from the eyepatch and back to the reality of the "miracle of flight" we were about the experience. After ordering an orange juice for me and for the son sitting on my side of the aisle, I reached down in to my carry on, to pull out a small travel size vodka.

I realize this does not put me up for mother of the year. I seldom drink, especially not hard liquor before lunch. But I really hate to fly. I was wearing an eyepatch. Drinks on a plane cost more than I have in my IRA. So planning ahead, I had packed my own single serving of alcohol to add to the orange juice, which would ensure for a calmer mother in flight, and less of a dent in our bank account. The steward brought the orange juice, and after stealthily mixing the vodka in to my cup, I leaned down to close my bag and stow it in its safety approved position underneath the seat. As I sat back up, my heart stopped. My five year old in the seat next to me was happily playing with one of his toys, two orange juice cups sitting on his tray table. Two EMPTY cups. Trying to maintain my composure, I steadied by voice as my insides shook and asked "Sweetheart, did you drink mommy's orange juice?" Unfazed, he said a quick "Yes! I did!" and refocused his attention to the toy. The color draining out of my face, I pushed the button to call the steward.

After a moment that felt like days he came to see what we needed. "Yes, sir, I believe my son may have accidentally consumed my mixed drink." The steward, putting on his best I-am-not-going-to-judge-the-drunk-mother-pirate face, replied "Well how much did he drink? If you tell me what you ordered I can check with our team and see how much alcohol was in your beverage." I took a deep breath, swallowed what was left of my pride, and replied "Actually I packed my own alcohol and added it to the juice. But I think it was the equivalent of a shot." I am quite sure that I may have been the subject of this steward's after work stories for the rest of the week with his friends. To his credit he replied with a quiet, serious voice of discretion "Well let's get him a muffin." I spent the rest of the three hours in the flight with my hand on my son's stomach to monitor his breathing as he slept soundly. Various scenarios filled my mind of what would happen when we reached Oregon. Instead of being met by the picture ready family, my husband's parents would greet a disheveled daughter in law wearing an eye patch and escorting her five year old who was on his first bender after taking shots on a plane.

Our lives don't always live up to the magazine spread we create in our mind's eye. We make plans and work to ensure everything will go in a certain way, then we are disappointed. Inevitably the reality in front of us does not live up to the expectation we have pictured. We know that it is important to have goals, and that setting a standard of excellence in our lives can encourage us to try our hardest. There are very few people who stumble into achieving their dreams, and we are taught to picture success if we want to achieve it. But are we prepared to learn from our set backs and keep moving forward? Are we letting our desire for perfection get in the way of embracing the reality we are offered? What could we do if we accepted what is instead of longing for what we thought would be?

We know that some of these longings come from our constant connection to other people. We have a natural tendency to compare our lives with others. We may observe our relative depravity to someone else when we are invited to their home, or hear about their promotion. Or we reload our newsfeed to find pictures of our friends looking attractive and eating delicious meals in enviable vacation destinations. We see a friend's latest post with pictures of her family laying in the sun in the Caribbean eating fresh pineapple and salmon while we eat leftover cold macaroni and cheese out of a pot over the sink as the rain pelts our windows. We know deep down that our globe trotting friend has also eaten macaroni and cheese. But for that moment, our reality just doesn't compare. As we scroll through the pictures, we find ourselves dissatisfied.

Even if we are not discouraged by the lives of others, we may find ourselves disheartened simply by the vision we build each day based on our own standards. We wake up and look at the weather, or our schedule, or our email. We decide what the day will bring. We make plans and start creating the vision of our perfect reality. Then our event is rained out. Our appointment runs late and we don't get to the store. Our health fails and we end up back in bed. We get a curt response to an email we spent hours crafting the night before. The vision starts to dissolve in front of us and we are left wanting.

In Mark 14, we meet a woman who had no idea she would be in the Bible, studied for centuries after her life. By everyone's standards, she was hardly perfect. This was not a woman dressed effortlessly beautiful carrying blog worthy cookies and heading off to her successful job with her picture ready children walking obediently behind her. This was a woman with nothing to offer by all outside measures of success. But she gave everything she could. Let's take a look:

> Now the Passover and the Festival of Unleavened Bread were only two days away, and the chief priests and the teachers of the law were scheming to arrest Jesus secretly and kill him. "But not during the festival," they said, "or the people may riot. While he was in Bethany, reclining at the table in the home of Simon the Leper, a woman came with an alabaster jar of very expensive perfume, made of pure nard. She broke the jar and poured the perfume on his head. Some of those present were saying indignantly to one another, "Why this waste of perfume? It could have been sold for more than a year's wages and the money given to the poor." And they rebuked her harshly. "Leave her alone," said Jesus. "Why are you bothering her? She has done a beautiful thing to me. The poor you will always have with you, and you can help them any time you want. But you will not always have me. She did what she could. She poured perfume on my body beforehand to prepare for my burial. Truly I tell you, wherever the gospel is preached throughout the world, what she has done will also be told, in memory of her. (Mark 14:1-9, NRSV)

The woman we meet in the passage with Jesus was not perfect, which the disciples were quick to point out. When she heard about Jesus, she could have thought of a thousand reasons why she should stay away. What if he didn't want to see her? What if the disciples made fun of her? What if this was a huge mistake? In every scenario she could imagine in her head, none of them ended with a perfect moment. Her daily reality was a struggle, and the one thing of value she owned was her alabaster jar. The perfume in it was expensive, and she had been saving it for years. There were lots of things that could have been done with the money the perfume would have brought from a sale in the market. Maybe it would have been better to sell it, as the disciples said. Maybe she was crazy to think he would want her to anoint him. But something in her pushed past any objection she felt and right in to his presence.

She is walking toward Jesus, carrying the jar full of perfume. Her heart is pounding in her ears. She sees the disciples gathered around him. One of them looks at her suspiciously as she draws closer. Their conversation quiets as they all turn to watch her, and one of them stands. She knows she must act quickly before they try to send her away. She acts in one quick move, walking decisively toward Jesus and looking in to his eyes. As she breaks open the jar, its shards scatter across the floor and the thick, sweet smell of perfume fills the air as she pours it across his head. She holds her breath as the disciples shout at her in protest, but as she looks into the eyes of Jesus she doesn't see the condemnation of the disciples. She sees the beginning of a smile.

She saw Jesus and knew in that moment what to do. The text tells us "she did what she could." In fact, she gave everything she could, giving the perfume from her jar to anoint his head. Jesus claims her act was a preparation for the sacrifice that stands in the center of his ministry, the crucifixion. This woman embraced the reality that she had, the tools at her disposal, and in one bold moment not only anointed Jesus Christ but also became a part of the gospel story for the ages to come. Perfection was outside of her grasp. But living in to the calling before her was hers for the taking.

You have been given a moment to live in. It may not be the moment you planned on this morning, and it may pale in comparison to the plans you carefully constructed. You may find you resonate more with my adventure as a pirate than with your friend in the Caribbean. But who needs salmon and white sand beaches? (Okay, we wouldn't turn them away). This though is your day, your chance, your moment. You stand at the sink eating macaroni. You are there because there is someone who needed your time when you could have been eating and you chose to give it to them. You chose reality. You took a phone call from a friend who needed to talk, went on a quick errand for your sister who hasn't been well, or simply stopped for a moment with your child to draw dinosaurs together. Reality over perfection. You spoke up at work to challenge your team to think through the ethics of their proposal, even though you knew there was coffee spilled on your suit from the chaos of that morning's commute. Reality over perfection. You volunteered at the soup kitchen even though your most impressive recipe is slightly burnt toast and offered a helping hand to feed the hungry. Reality over perfection.

God, it turns out, is present in our every day, messy reality. God has a life for us to live and it will happen in those moments that are missed if we are looking for perfect days instead of for the living Christ. When we disembarked our plane, my in laws ran toward us, so excited to see their family, and threw their arms around us in a giant hug. They didn't care that we were a mess. They were just thrilled we were there to see them. I learned that day that the reality of the moment was more important than the expectation I formed. I also learned that my five year old could hold his liquor better than a college fraternity pledge.

The woman who anointed Jesus jumped in to her moment fully. She didn't hang back and wait to see what anyone would say. She didn't worry if she was doing it wrong. She just did it, knowing she would only have one chance to be that close to her Lord. This was her reality, and she chose to live it.

There were all sorts of people in the congregation where I worshipped just after college. Some were younger and some were well into retirement. The community was near the coast so while some came in suits and dresses, others came in flip flops and bermuda shorts. There was one woman who came each week without fail. She was in her sixties and life had not been kind to her. She was out of work and struggling to get by on government assistance for food and housing. She lived alone and never seemed to have family around. Her clothing was mismatched and a bit tattered, and the strain of her days showed in the wrinkles along her sun beaten face. The woman would sit alone on the side row, swaying to the worship songs and offering quiet prayers beneath her purple straw hat. Her health was not good enough to volunteer with the church's building programs or cooking ministries. She didn't sing in the choir or help in the nursery. But she was known for her cards. The woman never missed a birthday or anniversary. Armed with the church directory she would painstakingly handwrite notes to each member of the congregation and bring them a card on their special day. Many of the cards were slightly torn or missing an entire half, recycled from a previous use. But she didn't let the lack of perfection keep her from serving others. Each Sunday she would carry in her small pile and hand them out, one at a time. She could have stayed away because she didn't feel like she could dress fancy enough. She could have told herself she had nothing to offer this congregation. But instead she had a card ministry that reached out to people of all ages in our church, and we began to eagerly anticipate her cards on our holidays. Others might have sung from the stage or led the children's summer program, but only she remembered your birthday. Only this woman gave us a card every year. For some it was their favorite card in the pile they received. For others, it was the only card, the only person who remembered, and it held a place of honor on their refrigerator. She wasn't perfect. But she embraced her reality and offered what she could. She showed people, in her cards, that they mattered. She did what she could.

What would you do today if you knew this was your one chance to embrace what is before you? Who would you spend time with if you thought God was planning to use you in their life to do something no one else could? What would you do differently if whatever happened today is a place God can use you, even if things don't work out as you imagined? What would you do today if your goal was to hear God say about you, "she did what she could?"

Chapter 2
WISDOM OVER KNOWLEDGE
Styrofoam Sets and a Missing Mortician

During my junior year of high school, I had two things that occupied my time outside of classes. The first was academics. I was determined to do well in my courses, and I would use any free moments I had to perfect my latest paper or work ahead on a reading assignment. Many a Saturday was filled with coloring in the different sections of the digestive system or pulling out my hair over the latest proof for Calculus. The second was theater. I was hardly the star of our theater department, but I enjoyed the costumes and backstage antics even in my less than leading role of "chorus member number nine." There was a sense of camaraderie in the cast, as we worked together toward a common goal of excellence, or at least not humiliation, on opening night.

There was one particular boy in the cast, one year younger than I, who was both fantastically talented and completely obnoxious. He was the total package for theater, with a strong singing voice, expressive face and good memory for lines. Even better, he was one the few who had won the puberty lottery and had acquired an impressive height of over six feet, which in high school theater is as unique as skilled tap dancing. But there was something about him that drove me crazy. Maybe it was the way he would try to intimidate other students during auditions. While most of of us sat huddled nervously at the front of the cold auditorium, he sauntered in a few minutes late. He would then make a production of spreading out a large colorful Mexican blanket on the floor, where he would sit drinking coffee from a silver thermos, looking relaxed. Maybe it was his confidence, or that he always secured one of the leading roles. I developed a dislike for the talented sophomore and even went as far as to tell a friend that I believed he would never get married because no girl would be able to tolerate him.

The show preparations were intensifying as we neared opening night, with rehearsals after school running in to the evening hours, and even taking up the bulk of our Saturdays. We worked hard to keep the balance with academics as well, knowing that a failing grade would not only land us a week of grounding at home but also remove us from the play due to school extracurricular requirements. Our drama teacher, who took academics as seriously as the pending performance, had assigned an intense set design project due just a few days before the opening. I stayed up late in to the night, creating a three dimensional set. My hands were covered in styrofoam crumbs and paint, and I worked tirelessly to hang the tiny curtains in just the right places, and affix labels for each portion of the stage.

The next morning I carefully stowed the completed set underneath my desk in my first class of the day, AP English Literature. Just as the noise of the classroom faded away and we immersed ourselves in the Shakespearean reading, a knock came at the classroom door. In poked the head of none other than that boy from the play. He politely addressed our teacher and, to my surprise, indicated that they needed to see me in the front office. Checking to make sure my project was not bumped by my chair, I followed him out in to the hall.

But as I headed toward the office, he stopped me.
"They don't really need you in the office."
I said nothing, but looked quizzically at him.
"So you know how we have that drama project due today?" he asked, with a sheepish smile on his face and a sparkle in his eyes. Again, I waited silently to see where this conversation was headed.
"I know that you don't have a partner for yours."
This was true. I didn't. Partners only weigh you down, and I usually chose to do projects alone.
"Well, I didn't exactly get my project finished, and I was thinking maybe we could present your project together." My first instinct was the turn on my heel and march back in to class. Then I remembered. The play. If he didn't do the project, he failed the class. If he failed the class, he couldn't be in the play, which opened in just four days. What would we do without the lead? Looking back, I honestly don't know what made me do it, but as my brain cried out in righteous indignation, I heard my mouth say,
"Okay. See you in third period then."

The next hour went quickly and before I knew it I was standing in front of my drama class with the tall boy and my meticulously created set. I pointed out the measurements of the walls, and the labels for the different portions of the stage. Then, realizing he should say something to show he had been a part of the team, he said "And there are the curtains." There was an awkward silence punctuated by a few muffled giggles, and the drama teacher raised a suspicious eye brow, but said nothing. I had, after all, claimed him as my partner and his name appeared right below mine on the set. As we left class that day, I had mixed feelings. My conscious was conflicted over what I had done, and I wrestled with the ethics of my decision. My mind also peppered me with concerns. As a driven student, I took seriously the commitment to obtaining knowledge. How would the boy from theater learn more information if other students helped him as I had done? How would he survive in the world after high school without the facts I poured over in our textbooks?

We put a high value on information in our society. Our children are starting school younger every year, with flashcards available for infants to start their study of words. With our connections online we are no longer limited to the information available in our latest Encyclopedia Britannica, and we can find all the information we could want on the habitat of tube worms on the ocean floor or the price earnings ratio for Apple stock over the past decade. Some of our information is more accurate than others, but the sheer amount of information we are exposed to is growing every day. This availability of knowledge has affected how we live. Our children take national tests to see how much information they know. We only book a hotel room or buy a dishwasher after reading thousands of reviews. We can seek feedback from people all over the world on everything from child raising to investing for retirement. And we do.

Certainly knowledge in itself isn't bad. Knowledge educates us, challenges us, and helps us to make well informed decisions. But what if knowledge can't tell the whole story?

Take a look at this familiar story from the gospel of Luke, chapter 1:

> In the sixth month the angel Gabriel was sent by God to a town in Galilee called Nazareth, to a virgin engaged to a man whose name was Joseph, of the house of David. The virgin's name was Mary. And he came to her and said, "Greetings, favored one! The Lord is with you." But she was much perplexed by his words and pondered what sort of greeting this might be. The angel said to her, "Do not be afraid, Mary, for you have found favor with God. And now, you will conceive in your womb and bear a son, and you will name him Jesus. He will be great, and will be called the Son of the Most High, and the Lord God will give to him the throne of his ancestor David. He will reign over the house of Jacob forever, and of his kingdom there will be no end." Mary said to the angel, "How can this be, since I am a virgin?" The angel said to her, "The Holy Spirit will come upon you, and the power of the Most High will overshadow you; therefore the child to be born will be holy; he will be called Son of God. And now, your relative Elizabeth in her old age has also conceived a son; and this is the sixth month for her who was said to be barren. For nothing will be impossible with God." Then Mary said, "Here am I, the servant of the Lord; let it be

with me according to your word." Then the angel departed from her. In those days Mary set out and went with haste to a Judean town in the hill country, where she entered the house of Zechariah and greeted Elizabeth. When Elizabeth heard Mary's greeting, the child leaped in her womb. And Elizabeth was filled with the Holy Spirit and exclaimed with a loud cry, "Blessed are you among women, and blessed is the fruit of your womb. And why has this happened to me, that the mother of my Lord comes to me? For as soon as I heard the sound of your greeting, the child in my womb leaped for joy. And blessed is she who believed that there would be a fulfillment of what was spoken to her by the Lord." And Mary said, "My soul magnifies the Lord, and my spirit rejoices in God my Savior, for he has looked with favor on the lowliness of his servant. Surely, from now on all generations will call me blessed;for the Mighty One has done great things for me and holy is his name. His mercy is for those who fear him from generation to generation. He has shown strength with his arm; he has scattered the proud in the thoughts of their hearts. He has brought down the powerful from their thrones, and lifted up the lowly; he has filled the hungry with good things, and sent the rich away empty. He has helped his servant Israel, in remembrance of his mercy, according to the promise he made to our ancestors, to Abraham and to his descendants forever." And Mary remained with her about three months and then returned to her home. (Luke 1:26-56, NRSV)

From all outward appearances, Mary was not someone who had a great deal of information. She did not have access to the kind of schooling our youth do today. Mary had not taken classes in biology or physics or algebra. She was a teenager who did not have the years of experiential knowledge to prepare her for this encounter with the angel. It is arguable that there is no amount of experience that could prepare someone for such an event. What Mary did know was that she was engaged to a man named Joseph, and they had plans to be married. But for her, everything else was about to change.

Mary's seemingly normal existence is interrupted by the appearance of an angel, who tells her not only will she have a child, but that this child will be the Son of God. What was Mary thinking as the angel spoke? Mary asks only one question for clarification of how she would become pregnant. As the angel finishes the proclamation, this young woman, who has had everything she knew called in to question, simply responds "Here I am, a servant of the Lord. Let it be with me according to your word." Mary makes a trip to see her friend Elizabeth, and this part of her story ends with her song of joy and praise to God.

She must have had a million questions. How would it be possible to be pregnant while she was still a virgin? Why, of all the women on earth, had God chosen her? What would happen once the child was born? What would Joseph say when he found out? What would her friends think? Would anyone believe her story? For such a key moment in her life, Mary had very little information. The angel had not given her the specifics of how all of this would come to be. Mary certainly couldn't do a web search to find information on pregnancy, or how to tell your fiancé that you are pregnant with the son of God. Mary does, however, appear to have the wisdom she needs for the task ahead of her. She seems to understand in a way that is shocking given her age and experience what God is doing within her, and what it might mean in the generations to come. Instead of asking a series of questions she listens to the angel, and then to the others that visit with her, and the text tells us later she "treasures these things in her heart." For Mary, wisdom was able to sustain her when knowledge could not. Knowledge was helpful, but wisdom was essential for her to face what lay ahead.

You have opportunities everyday to obtain knowledge. Receiving information helps you to grow in your understanding of the world and the people you share it with. Information enables you to function in society, to do your job, to handle the demands of living in a society with taxes, traffic laws and education. The big decisions in your life, however, cannot be made based purely on this knowledge. A pro and con list will only get you so far. If information alone could make fool proof choices then there would be little to separate us from the computers we rely on throughout our day. Wisdom, like Mary had, can help you decide what the right choice is in your life. Knowledge gives you all of the facts. Wisdom guides you to listen to your life, weigh the information available to you, and make a decision as you listen for the guidance of the Holy Spirit.

Knowledge is obtained. Wisdom is sought. Be warned though that seeking wisdom does not have the same appeal to our world as obtaining knowledge. Wisdom is hard to subject to a scientific method for proof. The ideas of "listening to your life" or "attending to the spirit" or "seeking counsel from others" are not straightforward or linear. Taking time to listen for the voice of God, to pray, to ask others for their perspectives may all lead to a wiser choice. But this perspective will not be as cut and dry as one developed from a textbook, and others may question your decision. They may see these concepts as weak compared to research for facts. Wisdom, however, is certainly not devoid of a quest for hard information. Choosing to seek wisdom in your life does not mean abandoning the resources available to you. A wise decision is not made purely on a gut feeling. Mary did ask a question of the angel and considered the information she was given. To chose wisdom then is to consciously fight to listen for God's leading through the Scripture, through others and through your experiences as you walk the path ahead fully informed and knowledgeable of the options available to you.

Our seeking of wisdom cannot be done in isolation. We need those around us, those with more experience to guide us on our way. As a part of our ministry training during seminary, we spent ten weeks working in a hospital to offer pastoral care. The experience was called CPE, Clinical Pastoral Education, and had a reputation for being the pastor's version of boot camp, minus the push ups. The hours were long and included overnights at the hospital. The emotional impact was intense as hour after hour was spent with suffering families and in trauma bays. What we had only read about in textbooks regarding suffering and death suddenly had names and hands and feet and the reality of it all was overwhelming. The time not spent in patient care was spent with a peer group of other students. During that time the supervisor would analyze our individual interactions with patients, delving in to our prejudices, past pains, and obstacles to emotional health. These conversations were as intense as any had in patient's rooms, and our group came to know one another with an intimacy one usually only finds at summer camp.

By the end of the first few weeks, we had a working knowledge of the hospital and its different departments. We got to know the staff, the fastest routes from one unit to another. We also learned how to find one another quickly by using our hospital beepers to locate our fellow students in the vast complex if we needed help. We were presented with binders full of information that we were to read and absorb to be competent in our work.

One afternoon our supervisor, the head chaplain, left the hospital in our hands for the evening. This was standard protocol, and we rehearsed together what was expected. We would respond to all trauma calls, check in on the various units, and, of course, be available in the case of any deaths. Just one hour after our supervisor left, my pager made its unmistakable chime. I dutifully headed to a phone and punched in the numbers glowing on my pager's screen. After a quick conversation with the front desk I learned that a family had arrived to view the body of their deceased relative. I took a deep breath. Nothing to worry about, I had all the knowledge I needed. I knew the procedure. I hung up and punched in the number for the morgue. We had been told that in the case of a viewing the mortician would take care of the details. There was no answer. The minutes were passing and I knew the family must be growing impatient. I quickly paged a fellow chaplain student who joined me on the elevator. We took it down in to the basement of the hospital and made our way toward the morgue entrance. The lighting was dim and as our eyes adjusted I shuddered slightly at the long tables that lined the halls. We sped up our pace and finally reached the sign marked "morgue." We banged on the gray metal door, but there was still no answer.

I took another deep breath. We knew the next step was to call security. We found a phone, asked security to fill in for the missing morgue team and headed to the room where we would meet the family. Minutes later, a large man in a security uniform entered, pushing a hospital gurney. But on the gurney was not a deceased loved one prepared for a viewing. It was a plain black body bag.

"Um, sir? Aren't you going to prep the um, deceased?"

He looked at me quizzically. "Lady, I just transport them. I don't prep them." And he left.

The door shut behind him and I felt panic rise in my throat. This was where my knowledge base ended. We had come to the end of the procedures list, and I was out of ideas. I paged another student. The three of us gathered around the deceased. In a moment of inspiration (stupidity), we had procured plastic gloves from the staff lounge. Somewhere in the land outside of knowledge and reason we had decided that the only option was that we would prepare the deceased for a viewing ourselves. We had neither the knowledge of how to do so nor the wisdom to know how silly we were to do something so outside of our experience. Just before we grabbed the edge of the zipper for the bag, one of my fellow students stopped. "The nurses!" She said suddenly. "They will know what to do!"

We approached the phone in the viewing room in two large strides and called the nursing station on the hospice floor. The nurse arrived in our room a few minutes later. She took one look at three chaplain students wearing medical gloves and suppressed a laugh. Looking back, we must have seemed ridiculous. But she didn't scold us. Her smile showed the wisdom of one who knew both the rashness facing death had inspired in us and the eagerness we held as young students hoping to succeed. We stepped out as she expertly arranged the body. When we returned with the family, the room no longer looked like a medical facility but a more appropriate funeral parlor. The nurse had worked her magic then left us to our attempts at pastoral care.

The knowledge of protocol had failed me. There was nothing in the my binder that could have prepared me for the evening's events. But I was not alone. I had the wisdom of a fellow student who knew we needed help. Even more we had the wisdom of the nurse, gained through experience and perspective, who saved what had felt like an impossible situation, and protected our sensitive egos in the process. Death and its practicalities had stumped me. I could not have faced that situation alone. Wisdom from the others around me had led the way when knowledge could not do so alone.

Knowledge will get us pretty far. But wisdom gives us the fuller picture. Thinking back to high school, the boy with the coffee and blanket who shared my project that day did manage to graduate from high school with all of the information he needed for college. Objective observation would have predicted that we would never have crossed paths again. Not even wisdom could have prepared me for what would happen next. Seventeen years later we are still happily married.

How would your life look different if you made a conscious effort to balance your time finding knowledge to also seeking wisdom? Who would you talk to as you considered your options? Is there someone who might be able to offer a better perspective than you currently have? How would your prayer life look different? What decisions are you currently facing that could be effected by a perspective of wisdom integrated with the information you have?

Chapter 3
HONESTY OVER COMFORT
Chicken Sandwich Ethics

My husband and I, deeply in love, were married relatively young. We were excited to start our lives together, and relished the first few months of setting up a home. We arranged and rearranged our three pieces of furniture in our tiny apartment living room, and enjoyed warm Florida evenings playing frisbee on the lawn. What we had in love, however, we lacked in financial resources. He was a senior in college, working part time in retail. I was working as an intern in a church, making less than a part time fast food cashier. There were some expenses we learned we couldn't control, like the electric bill. With others, like groceries, we invested our creativity to try to save money. We learned to live on peanut butter sandwiches and pasta, occasionally splurging on pizza. Items like avocado or mango were the things of dreams.

One morning we walked together to check the mail at the postage box for our apartment complex. Like most apartments, the mailboxes were clustered together in a few central locations throughout the property in a series of small locked containers. Just beside the mailboxes stood a large trash can for residents to dump their unwanted junk mail and advertisements. We inserted our key and opened our small metal box to find the normal bills waiting for us. But just underneath them was a flier. Before tossing it in the trash we took one last look at it and froze. This was not a flier, it was a coupon. Even better, it was not a coupon where you have to buy something to receive a discount. This was a coupon for several free items with no purchase necessary at a newly opening fast food restaurant in our town. In order to encourage business, the company had mailed out a flier which offered a free chicken sandwich, a free breakfast sandwich, and a free order of fries. No. Purchase. Necessary. It was manna from heaven. We started to rush off excitedly for the car to go pick up the best meal we would have had in a week. Then our eyes met, and I knew we were both thinking the same thing. The trash can. What if other residents had made the mistake we almost made, and tossed out the flier, thinking it to be a regular coupon or advertisement? Time stood still as we moved quickly back toward the trash can, eyeing it intently like a wild animal hunting its prey. We peered over the edge with hopeful anticipation. There, amongst the clothing advertisements and gum wrappers were more of the miracle coupons. Several of them. Without hesitation we plunged our hands in to the trash can, sorting out the fliers from the garbage. In a matter of minutes we had procured a week's worth of lunch. We looked at each other with giddy smiles on our faces and turned back toward home. As we walked we saw in the distance another mailbox cluster, with another trash can. This time we didn't need to say anything, but took off in a run toward the roofed mailbox area. This garbage can too produced several sandwich coupons. Over the next hour we moved from one mailbox area to another in our complex, coming home with a haul of no less than twenty four fliers.

That next month we ate like kings. During the day we subsisted on our normal peanut butter and toast, but each night for dinner we had another hot chicken sandwich. There was a luxury to having the guarantee of a large dinner each night, and it made us hungry to take things a step farther. Until that month, feeding ourselves had been a difficult but essential part of money management. Treating someone else to a meal had been impossible. We counted the breakfast sandwich coupons and decided to seize the opportunity. A few quick phone calls and we assembled the entire youth group we worked with to take them out to breakfast, on us. Or more accurately, on the salvaged coupons. The manager happened to be on the register that morning, and looked curiously at us as we presented 24 coupons and ordered 24 free breakfast biscuits. "How did you manage to end up with 24 of these coupons?" he asked. We had not anticipated the question. Until that point, we had been unnoticed in our free food bonanza. It wasn't like we had done anything wrong. But still, we faced a decision. Although we had enjoyed our garbage hunting adventure, when the story was said out loud it sounded not as impressive, even pathetic. We knew honesty was the right decision, especially as the eyes of our youth group were now fixed on us, waiting to see what we would do. The story poured out of us to the manager, of how we had found the one coupon in our mailbox, but then hunted for more. He paused when we finished, and then said "Well, that wasn't the way the coupons were intended to be used." He looked at the two of us, and at the eager faces of the teenagers behind us. Then he turned and put in the order for the twenty four breakfast sandwiches.

We have all had those moments. We are faced with the choice between sharing the truth and facing the potential consequences or telling a lie and softening the blow. Sometimes we convince ourselves that the lie is a better choice in order to avoid upsetting someone else. It is easier to say "of course I love how you look in that shirt." And perhaps in this case the truth is best, at least in part, softened in a symphony of softer words to diminish the chance one opinion, no matter how true, might be heard. But in other cases the choice between honesty and comfort becomes much more complicated. We worry the truth will cost us the relationship, and several days later we are caught in a tangled web of half truths. We justify our lies as not there for our own comfort but instead to avoid controversy at work, or to keep the peace in our homes. Perhaps the hardest of all are the lies we tell to ourselves. What harm is there in choosing comfort over honesty when the voice is only in our heads? Why not let ourselves believe what is easy instead of what is true? Why chose honesty when the truth is so uncomfortable?

The woman at the well had every reason to tell a few lies. Her life was not one she was proud of. We find her story in John 4:6-30:

> Jacob's well was there, and Jesus, tired out by his journey, was sitting by the well. It was about noon. A Samaritan woman came to draw water, and Jesus said to her, 'Give me a drink'. (His disciples had gone to the city to buy food.) The Samaritan woman said to him, 'How is it that you, a Jew, ask a drink of me, a woman of Samaria?' (Jews do not share things in common with Samaritans.) Jesus answered her, 'If you knew the gift of God, and who it is that is saying to you, "Give me a drink", you would have asked him, and he would have given you living water.' The woman said to him, 'Sir, you have no bucket, and the well is deep. Where do you get that living water? Are you greater than our ancestor Jacob, who gave us the well, and with his sons and his flocks drank from it?' Jesus said to her, 'Everyone who drinks of this water will be thirsty again, but those who drink of the water that I will give them will never be thirsty. The water that I will give will become in them a spring of water gushing up to eternal life.' The woman said to him, 'Sir, give me this water, so that I may never be thirsty or have to keep coming here to draw water.' Jesus said to her, 'Go, call your husband, and come back.' The woman answered him, 'I have no husband.' Jesus said to her, 'You are right in saying, "I have no husband"; for you have had five husbands, and the one you have now is not your husband. What you have said is true!' The woman said to him, 'Sir, I see that you are a prophet. Our ancestors worshipped on this mountain, but you say that the place where people must worship is in Jerusalem.' Jesus said to her, 'Woman, believe me, the hour is coming when you will worship the Father neither on this mountain nor in Jerusalem. You worship what you do not know; we worship what we know, for salvation is from the Jews. But the hour is coming, and is now here, when the true worshippers will worship the Father in spirit and truth, for the Father seeks such as these to worship him. God is spirit, and those who worship him must worship in spirit and truth.' The woman said to him, 'I know that Messiah is coming' (who is called Christ). 'When he comes, he

will proclaim all things to us.' Jesus said to her, 'I am he, the one who is speaking to you.' Just then his disciples came. They were astonished that he was speaking with a woman, but no one said, 'What do you want?' or, 'Why are you speaking with her?' Then the woman left her water-jar and went back to the city. She said to the people, 'Come and see a man who told me everything I have ever done! He cannot be the Messiah, can he?' They left the city and were on their way to him. (NRSV)

The woman insists on honesty from the beginning of her conversation with Jesus. She knew Jesus was Jewish and that it was not customary for the Jews to associate with someone like her, a Samaritan. When he asks her for a drink she could have neglected to tell him. It wasn't even a lie, just an omission. But she starts the conversation on a foundation of absolute truth.

As they talk, Jesus asks her to call her husband, and again she choses the harder way. She could have made up a million stories, claiming her husband was away or not well. Instead she is truthful, saying directly "I have no husband." Jesus responds with an honesty that matches her own, sharing what he knows of her life of promiscuity. She doesn't protest or try to explain away this blunt depiction of her life. Instead she is simply astounded that he knows her. Here is a Jewish man, sitting at the well, and he really knows her. He knows what she has done, and what her life really has been like over the past several years. Even more amazing, this man who claims to be the Messiah has not turned her away for her indiscretion but has welcomed her to sit and talk with him.

The woman does not hesitate after her talk with Jesus. She abandons her water jar and runs to the town, telling anyone who will listen about her conversation. She shouts down the streets that she has met a man who could be the Messiah. Then she does something that seems either very brave or absolutely crazy. She invites them to come and "see a man who told me everything I ever did." The people of the town must have known pieces of the woman's story. No doubt she was the subject of gossip in the square as she appeared with a different man so frequently throughout the years. The latest story circulating among the town people was that she was even living with a man now outside of marriage. She would have had every reason to hide, to keep her head down and try to deny the truth of her life. Here was a man who really knew what she had done, not just as heresay from the hushed whispers of the others. Anyone else might have walked quickly back home and hoped the man who spoke honesty about her life would leave and move on to another well. But not this woman. Her comfort was not her top concern. This man who spoke truth to her, this man who might be the Messiah, was someone she wanted everyone to meet.

You may have things in your life, like this woman, of which you are not proud. There may be things you are doing that you would like to sweep under the rug, to explain away, or to even lie to hide. The truth about what you have done is just too uncomfortable to bear. Or maybe you know there is an area of your life where you are not being completely honest. You know it is gray area, and you are hoping that if you just wait long enough the situation will go away and you can avoid the uncomfortable conversation that honesty would require.

The woman at the well had these things too. But she made a choice. She chose Jesus. The freedom she found in drawing close to Jesus far surpassed the discomfort of revealing the truth of her actions. She could not have known at the time the depth of the grace this man had to offer. She could not have realized fully that this strange and perceptive man not only offered truth but an overwhelming love that could change her to the core. In that moment the woman at the well opened her life to the Messiah and became an evangelist.

You have information that the woman at the well did not. You have heard the stories of Jesus, how he drew closest to sinners and offered a fresh start in their lives. Honesty may not be the popular choice, but when you are honest you open the way for God to come in to your life, to be truly known. There is a freedom that comes when you are honest not only with others, but with yourself. What a relief to realize that we are good enough, just as we are, to come to Jesus. What is required is not a clean history or a perfect life but only an honest heart.

Sometimes honesty costs us very little, like that morning in Chic-fil-A. The worst we could have lost were a stack of breakfast sandwiches and the gratefulness of a group of hungry teens. Sometimes honesty asks us to give up the sense of self we have carefully constructed in our mind. Honesty may ask us to risk our success, our fortune, our comfort. But it offers us the things we really crave in return. Our deceit buys us comfort at the cost of being fully known and accepted just as we are. Our honesty frees us to live in a true relationship with one another, and with God. Not as the person we imagine ourselves to be, but just as we are.

As we traveled one summer in Portland, we met a young woman who was still in high school. She was only a few weeks in to her relationship with the young man next to her, but there was a casual ease between the two of them that indicated a maturity far beyond their age and the length of the time together. They seemed to speak their minds directly to one another, and their interaction was absent of the manipulation I so often associate with couples, especially those formed in adolescence. When she indicated the newness of their relationship, I responded with this observation of the perceived depth between them. She said they had simply decided to be honest, all the time. If something bothered them, they said so. If they appreciated what the other had said, they shared their appreciation. If they didn't want to do a certain activity or if they had made a misstep, they shared it without hesitation. Open communication was essential for them, even when it was hard. In this, she said, they found a freedom from the exhaustive games of early courtship. They could simply be exactly who they are as individuals, but together. I was astounded by the wisdom of this young woman, who knew at 17 what I was only realizing in my thirties.

Most of us want to be honest, and the best place to start is with our own lives. Before we can be open with someone else, we must first take stock. For some of us, this means addressing the lies we have told ourselves, that the behaviors we have been hiding are really not a problem, that we could stop anytime we wanted to. Honesty might start at admitting there is a problem and that we are really might need help. It might mean choosing to expose to ourselves the destructiveness of our choices. For others, the lies are in the form of self degradation, that we are not beautiful or smart or capable. These second lies are easier to overlook because they mask themselves as humility. But lies that tear down our image as children of God are as dangerous as the lies we use to justify unhealthy behavior. The same Jesus who met the woman at the well, the same Jesus who says "go and sin no more," meets you, sharing the truth that you are beautiful and loved, just as you are, as a child of God.

As we chose honesty with ourselves, it opens us up to be honest with God. If we can stop hiding the truth of our struggles from ourselves, we can lay them before God and begin to heal. As we take these next steps with God, we are then open to be honest with others. One day at a time, we find that the short term discomfort honesty requires transforms our relationships.

What would your life look like if you chose honesty over comfort? How would your relationships be different? What would this honesty cost you, but what would you have to gain? How could it change your relationship with those closest to you, and your relationship with God?

Chapter 4
HOPE OVER DESPAIR
Refrigerator Graffiti

In September of 2013 my son was hit by a car. It was one of those moments that unfolded in slow motion. We were walking home from school and a car turned the corner just as we crossed the street. My younger son and I jumped backward to avoid it, but my older son jumped forward to try and make it to the sidewalk. He fell to the ground and the car went up over his ankle. It was no one's fault. It could have happened to anyone. It did happen to us.

Much of the next few minutes were a blur. I dropped to the ground next to him and held my face inches from his, singing a song I sang when he was a baby. Our eyes locked and we talked softly to one another. A crowd had gathered and without breaking from his gaze I handed my phone back to the first set of hands I found and asked them to call the paramedics. We took the ambulance to children's hospital. As his body tried to go in to shock, his mind resisted, focusing on the conversations around him. We did math problems, which he loves, to keep him alert. After a multitude of X-rays and a substantial dose of pain killers, we took him home, with a large plaster traction cast running from his ankle to his hip. His leg was too heavy to lift and he would need a wheel chair for several weeks, before progressing to crutches and then to a brace.

Our days took on a new rhythm. School and work and playdates were replaced with doctor's appointments and therapy. Our living room was transformed in to a study, a bedroom and a dining room so we could live on the first floor. Goals for homework gave way to goals of learning to use a wheelchair and then crutches, and then learning to walk again. Each evening after getting the kids to sleep, my husband and I would whisper to one another on the kitchen floor, yards away from where he slept. We were flooded with emotion. Deep gratitude that he wasn't killed or more severely injured. Shock that it had happened at all. Grief for our son who would have a long road of healing ahead. A general free floating anger with no one person to blame.

The next few months were hard. On top of the pain of a very broken leg, he had surgery for a ruptured appendix and several other complications. Just as he was walking again, he refractured the leg and was back in a brace. Spikes in pain or unexpected flights of stairs could derail a day. An understanding friend or meal on our doorstep could put one back together. As a pastor who has spent a decent amount of time reflecting on questions like "why do bad things happen?" I couldn't ascribe the suffering of my son to some preordained plan of God. I do not believe God runs children over with cars to accomplish a certain purpose written in the stars, anymore than I believe God gives children cancer or burns down their homes. I knew intellectually that God was there with us, but I felt like my spirit was grasping in the silence. If there wasn't a preordained reason, then the suffering was meaningless. If this hadn't happened for a purpose, than how could anything good possibly come of it? The darkness of the late nights were when exhaustion and despair carried their strongest punch, as I strained to hear God's voice without success.

In those weeks, one Scripture clawed its way in to my heart. "Suffering produces endurance, endurance produces character and character produces hope. And hope does not disappoint us." (Romans 5:3-4, NRSV) I didn't know if I could even believe it was true at the time. I took some chalk and wrote the verse on the chalkboard painted front of our refrigerator. I was uncertain of its truth for us, but somehow seeing it in print seemed to make it more possible. Each day the verse seemed to stake a deeper claim on our lives, or at least in our kitchen. Even when we felt like life was just too difficult, hope demanded a space in our home. There was something about hope that had a strong pull for me. Happiness felt too wishy washy. We had no room for laughter or smiles when he was in such pain. Strength was assumed because weakness wasn't an option. Grief was ever present but we were fighting to fully give in to it. But we could cling to hope. We hoped for a better day tomorrow than today. We hoped for healing, both physical and emotional, in our home. We hoped for God to be working goodness, the things of character and endurance, through the suffering. We hoped that someday we would be able to use what we were learning to help someone else. We hoped we could hold it together for another minute, then another hour. We cried and we prayed and we worked. And we hoped. And we were not disappointed.

The suffering was no less real. Growing bones in painful work, and healing from traumatic experiences may be even harder. But soon there was a list of successes on the refrigerator, next to the verse written in pink chalk, that we would update each day. No matter how small, each day had something we could cling to that had been accomplished. One day we were given a ramp for the front steps. Another we figured out how to get to the car through the rain. One day we laughed for the first time since the accident. One day at a time, we found hope.

Life, for all of us, in one way or another, is hard. Some of us have it harder than others. As we sat in hospital rooms in to the early hours of the morning that year, I found myself noticing others who did not have the same outcome of healing we could look toward. For these families, their children were on the beginning of a lifetime of illness. Some would never take their children home. Where, I wondered, would they find hope, when we struggled even knowing life would get better in the months to come?

No matter what struggles we face, we all face times when despair threatens to overtake us, drowning out any chance of hope. If it is not a sick child, it is a lost job. Financial instability. Strained family relationships. A divorce or difficult break up. A miscarriage or infertility. The death of a loved one. The grief of lost dreams. Some of our troubles are temporary, and the despair comes and goes over a period of hours. Other times we face a path with an unknown destination, and the despair lingers day in and day out like a stray cat that is never satisfied.

We are not alone. The woman in the eighth chapter of the gospel of Luke is not given a name. She shows up for only a few verses, but her suffering is described in detail. For twelve years this woman has suffered. She had an illness that had made her bleed for over a decade. She had been to healers and doctors and others who made promises and offered false hope, but still her condition lingered on. Her bleeding ostracized her from the community, for she was considered unclean. Not only had she lost her health, but her friends, her life. Those who hadn't abandoned her for the social stigma she carried had gradually grown weary of her suffering and distanced themselves. She walked the streets that day, weak and exhausted and alone, and noticed a crowd was gathering. As people rushed past her she heard pieces of their conversations. They talked of Jesus, who had done miraculous healings for others. Jesus, who was believed by some to be the Son of God. He was here, he was walking through her town, down her street. She joined the throng of people pushing to get close to him. She was used to staying unnoticed, and she slipped quietly between the people in front of her, keeping her eyes on his cloak that was dragging on the dusty road just feet ahead of her. As the crowd jostled her forward she drew a deep breath and closed her eyes. For years she had fought against the despair, sometimes so deep she wanted to die. Everyday had been struggle but she had refused to give up, holding on to the seemingly impossible hope that she could make tomorrow better. Something about this man had given her a jolt of new strength. As she let out her breath she reached forward a shaking, pale hand and touched the edge of his cloak. In that moment, she felt something change within her. It felt like an electric current had moved through her body. She felt . . . different. She felt whole. It couldn't be true. But it was. She was healed. Her bleeding was stopped.

> "Then Jesus asked, 'Who touched me?' When all denied it, Peter* said, 'Master, the crowds surround you and press in on you.' But Jesus said, 'Someone touched me; for I noticed that power had gone out from me.' When the woman saw that she could not remain hidden, she came trembling; and falling down before him, she declared in the presence of all the people why she had touched him, and how she had been immediately healed. He said to her, 'Daughter, your faith has made you well; go in peace.' Luke 5:45-48 (NRSV)

We know it doesn't always work out this way. Sometimes the miracle comes, like it did for the woman in the crowds that afternoon. But other times we pray and beg and cry out to God for healing and things seem to stay the same. We try to reach the edge of Jesus' cloak and are instead shuffled aside by the crowds. People try to explain why we haven't had a miracle. We are told if we just pray harder, if we just believe more, then it will change. People grow weary of our suffering. They look for answers in our behavior or our diet or our lifestyle. They blame our lack of faith.

A lack of healing is not due to a lack of faith. God has not necessarily ordained this episode of pain for your life. Sometimes, more often than not, suffering just happens. We suffer because we live in bodies of flesh and blood that are fragile and feel pain. Or we suffer because the world is full of sinful people who make sinful choices that affect each of us. We also suffer for reasons we cannot possibly identify or understand. There have been books and articles written to explain the problem of suffering but at the end of the day they fall short. Only God understands the mystery of suffering and evil in the world. We still want a reason almost as much as we want healing, but we are often left disappointed on both counts.

So why do we chose hope over despair? Because it is the only thing that can sustain us. Remember again the verse from Romans. Suffering produced endurance and endurance produces character and character produces hope. And hope does not disappoint us. Hope doesn't promise that suffering will go away. Hope says that even though things are hard, that God is there, right in the middle of it. Despair says that you are alone. Hope says that God will give you the endurance to get through the next obstacle. Despair says you are too weak to go another day. Hope says that things will get better, either in this life or the life to come. Despair says this life is all there is. Despair makes a convincing argument. But even in our darkest hour, hope doesn't give up. At the end of the day, hope wins. Because hope comes from a God who loves us and stands with us, especially in suffering. Hope doesn't disappoint because it is rooted in the God who doesn't make promises that won't come to pass. Hope is the star in the night sky, that even when it isn't visible, is always there, shining in the dark.

Sometimes hope comes to us. Sometimes we have to go looking for it. There was an older couple in the church a few years back that had been through a lot together. Their love was obvious in the gentle way he would touch her hand, the way she looked in his eyes. They had lived through many great years together, raising children, celebrating grandchildren, and now living in retirement much earned after the hard work of the past few decades. But over the past few years life had taken a turn and she became ill. He stood by her bedside, offering care and companionship, but after several months of decline she passed away. It was a Saturday. Grief filled the air of his home. There was a palpable absence around him. His best friend, his lover, his companion, his wife. Gone. Everything in the home was a reminder of her. He walked by the closet and turned quickly away. Her clothes still hung there, pressed and neat on hangers all in a row, like nothing had changed. But everything had changed. Finally the day gave way in to the night, and he slept fitfully. The next morning as the sun broke the sky, he swung his feet gently off the bed and padded on to the carpet. His body felt heavy and his mind was clouded with exhaustion and grief. Slowly he forced himself to put his hands through his shirt sleeves, slip on his dress pants, and tie his shoes. He slipped on his tie and flattened it neatly on his shirt as he had countless times before. A friend pulled in to the driveway and he walked to the car, his eyes still red with dark circles beneath them. He arrived and received the embrace of one friend after another as he made his way to the familiar small room behind the sanctuary. There he slipped his arms into the heavy red fabric of his choir robe and lined up to process in to the church. Behind him, another man placed a hand on his shoulder and gave it a small squeeze. That morning, just hours after the death of his wife, he sang in the choir on Sunday morning. The despair was real. But he clung tightly to hope.

You have had, or are currently experiencing, real hardship in your life. God offers you something more powerful than the most difficult situation you face. This is not the weak hope of romantic comedies. It is not the temporary hope of a spring day. This is tough, gritty, powerful hope that forces light in to the darkest hour of your life and surrounds you. It is all encompassing and doesn't make false promises of an easy road ahead. It is a hope that can only develop out of the experience of suffering, and is the welcome byproduct of endurance and character. What would change in your life if you sought out this hope that God offers? How would it change how you approach times of hardship? How can you offer hope, instead of grasping explanations, to someone who is struggling in your life?

Chapter 5
OPENNESS OVER FAMILIARITY
Treehouse Hippies and the Temple

Treehouses are a fascination of mine. Growing up, I was a very cautious kid. I marveled at the others who could climb trees. They would throw their arms and legs around the trunk in a sort of hug and rise quickly in to the canopy of leaves, pieces of bark tumbling down behind them. I would gaze up after them until all I could see were dirty bare feet dangling as they straddled a secure branch, perched high above the ground. I never had a treehouse, but I loved the idea that one could climb a ladder and hide out high above the world, peering out above the tree tops.

When I was in my twenties I had my opportunity. On a short road trip north with my husband, we were looking for a place to stay for the night. Stowed in the side pocket of the car door, beside gum wrappers and dollar store sunglasses was a book listing hostels around the country. Flipping casually through the options, one title jumped off the page. It was a hostel in a forest. The rooms were all tree houses. My imagination filled with the desires of my youth. I pictured swaying rope ladders ascending toward the sky. I could see the worn wooden slats. Perhaps the tree house would have bunk beds or even a telescope. How else would be watch out for pirates? Tonight it would finally happen. Tonight I would sleep up in the trees.

Just a few hours later we turned off the interstate and began the trek down a bumpy dirt road, meant more for an off road four by four than our Honda sedan. The car bounced and bumped its way down through the forest, sending clouds of dust in to the air in its wake. There was a break in the clearing ahead, and my eyes lit up. Just visible through the dust and foliage were several tree houses, high above the ground.

The treehouse was exactly as I had dreamed. There was a small wooden ladder leading in to a trap door. The platform was nestled perfectly among the branches, with the strong tree trunk standing as the center of the room. But the treehouse wasn't the only thing visible in the clearing. There were people wandering on the grounds in the woods. The people seemed to be a part of a sort of commune that lived at the hostel, and they were unlike any other people I had seen before. The community were I grew up in Florida had all sorts of different people from every race and demographic. The schools I attended as a child represented this diversity. But these individuals were different than any of those. It had nothing to do with the boxes one finds on a population survey. It wasn't their age or race or class. It was something they had, or rather didn't have, that set them apart. They were . . . naked.

I grew up in a modest home. We changed in our rooms and kept the bathroom door shut. In locker rooms in middle school we had invented ways to change through a system of layers of clothing and a feat of acrobatics that maintained this privacy. Until that moment, the idea that someone would be anywhere outside of a shower without clothing seemed as possible as Santa Claus joining me for a sushi dinner in the Bahamas. And yet there, ahead of me on the path, stood the man. A naked man. He was in his fifties and had a mustache and beard covering his face, and his hair fell almost to his shoulders. He was standing in the afternoon sun, a peaceful look on his face as he stretched his arms up toward the sky. Squinting in to the sunlight he caught a glimpse of us standing there. I closed my eyes then opened them again, wondering if I had imagined him. A smile broke out on his face and he gave a eager friendly wave, stretched again, then sauntered off down the path in the other direction.

I was momentarily frozen in place, stunned. In all of my imaginings of tree houses, things had come and gone. Sometimes they had walls, other times they were a simple platform. Somethings they had beds, and other times a nook for reading in a chair. But one thing never changed. Everyone had always been clothed. My feet unglued themselves from the spot where I was rooted and we continued down the path to find the office to check in. The woman at the desk was friendly (and thankfully dressed) and we left minutes later with directions to our tree house for the night.

We set off down the path and saw the reflection of water glimmering on the trunks of several trees. The reflection was coming from a natural pool. It was really just a hole dug in the ground and full of water, but it served its purpose of offering a respite from the summer heat. A decent crowd laughed and splashed together. We drew closer and realized these others were, like the man, free of the clothing we felt to be common in mixed company. They seemed unconcerned and relaxed, leaning against the muddy edges of the pool. Occasionally one of them would rise from the waters and stand on the edge, their skin glistening in the light that filtered through the trees, then jump back in to splash the others.

I gripped my backpack a little tighter and scampered quickly down a side path that led deeper in to the woods. We passed a small group of chickens in a pen, scratching in the dirt and pecking at the food on the ground. There was also a small vegetable patch near the building that served as a common dining hall. As I neared the ladder for our site, I breathed a sigh of relief. There was something disconcerting about the others in the forest that afternoon. It went against everything I had grown up understanding to be proper. As a young adult, I considered myself open to the world and its people. I had not realized how set in my ways I was until I encountered a group so different from myself. How was it that these people could run about in the forest, without care for their lack of modesty? Did they go to jobs and have cars, or did they live here, off the grid of normal society, eating from the garden and swimming away the warm afternoons? Where did they come from that they were so comfortable with this way of life that seemed so foreign to me? I quickly scaled up the ladder to our tree house and sunk gratefully on to the floor, relieved to have several feet between me and the ground and the naked hippies.

We are comfortable with what is familiar. We see many of the same people and places in our routines. We drive the same route to work. We shop at the same grocery store. We develop a circle of friends and family with whom we socialize. Within this familiarity, our perspective on reality is shaped and we become comfortable with what we see around us. The world becomes defined by what we experience in our own small piece of existence. But what happens when we are challenged to see something outside of our small piece of the earth? What happens when our eyes are opened to something new?

Anna's life had been confined to the familiar walls of the temple for years. After she become a widow at a young age, she had stayed in this holy place. The familiarity of the room was comforting and the routine soothed her. Somedays she would pray for hours, the silence punctuated by the devout coming to offer acts of worship. Many days she fasted, listening carefully for the word of God as a prophet. Anna had reached an age of 84, and had seen a lot in her time. Now her days took on a regular rhythm in her world defined by the temple.

But one day things changed. A young couple approached, carrying a small boy. It was Mary and Joseph, and the child carefully wrapped in Mary's arms was Jesus. Anna gazed at the couple and knew her eyes had been opened. She knew that this was not just another couple coming to the temple. This was not the ordinary act of worship that was required. This couple would change her reality, her perspective, as none had done before:

> When the time came for their purification according to the law of Moses, they brought him up to Jerusalem to present him to the Lord as it is written in the law of the Lord, 'Every firstborn male shall be

designated as holy to the Lord'), and they offered a sacrifice according to what is stated in the law of the Lord, 'a pair of turtle-doves or two young pigeons.' (Luke 2:22-24, NRSV)

Before Anna could approach them, she saw Simeon, and knew he must see something different about them too.

Now there was a man in Jerusalem whose name was Simeon;˙ this man was righteous and devout, looking forward to the consolation of Israel, and the Holy Spirit rested on him. ˙t had been revealed to him by the Holy Spirit that he would not see death before he had seen the Lord's Messiah.˙ Guided by the Spirit, Simeon˙ came into the temple; and when the parents brought in the child Jesus, to do for him what was customary under the law, Simeon˙ took him in his arms and praised God, saying,
'Master, now you are dismissing your servant˙ in peace,
  according to your word;
for my eyes have seen your salvation,
  which you have prepared in the presence of all peoples,
a light for revelation to the Gentiles
  and for glory to your people Israel.

And the child's father and mother were amazed at what was being said about him. Then Simeon˙ blessed them and said to his mother Mary, 'This child is destined for the falling and the rising of many in Israel, and to be a sign that will be opposed so that the inner thoughts of many will be revealed—and a sword will pierce your own soul too.' (Luke 2:25-35, NRSV)

Anna felt a rush in her spirit. She thought at 84 she had seen everything. But there before her, in the temple, the couple stood. She felt the rush of God's presence within her and her heart swelled with joy. This child was indeed the Messiah:

There was also a prophet, Anna˙ the daughter of Phanuel, of the tribe of Asher. She was of a great age, having lived with her husband for seven years after her marriage, then as a widow to the age of eighty-four. She never left the temple but worshipped there with fasting and prayer night and day. At that moment she came, and began to praise God and to speak about the child˙ to all who were looking for the redemption of Jerusalem.

When they had finished everything required by the law of the Lord, they returned to Galilee, to their own town of Nazareth. The child grew and became strong, filled with wisdom; and the favor of God was upon him. (Luke 2:36-40, NRSV)

For years Anna had been in the temple. She would have had every reason to ignore the couple who entered, to shove aside the stirring in her spirit. There was little she hadn't seen in her years of fasting and prayer, why should today be different? Anna could have closed her eyes to the new reality in front of her, and pulled back in to the shadows of the comfort of the familiar. But she didn't. Anna's eyes were opened to a new thing God was doing in the world. Instead of responding with fear or hesitation, she ran forward to embrace it, she sought to understand it. Anna chose, in that moment, openness over familiarity.

You have the choice to do this everyday. Even in the familiarity of your routine, you will encounter people or situations that are outside the comfort of what you know and understand. The world and its people continue to change and you will have the opportunity to see God at work in and among them. Maybe you will find yourself in a conversation with someone who has a perspective different from your own. Maybe you will take a wrong turn and end up in a new part of your town. In these unexpected moments, God offers you the opportunity to open your eyes and expand your vision of God's people.

But we have to make the choice. It is all too easy to chose to shut our eyes to that which we don't understand or recognize or agree. The familiar calls us back to what we know and we retreat in to circles of people who won't challenge us. We turn off the news when we hear something that might call us to change. We spend time with people who we know share our political or religious preferences. We struggle to stay when we are uncomfortable.

We stayed in the forest that night. Not because we are a living example of openness, but because we needed a place to sleep. The sky darkened and we laid in our tree house, the noises of chickens scratching in the darkness filling the evening air. The next morning I left the hostel appearing just as I had arrived. Clothed. But admittedly over the past twenty four hours I had gained an appreciation for their way of life. They seemed so relaxed and free of the trappings of society. They weren't worried about being late for an appointment or frustrated by the long line at the drive through. They ate the food they could grow themselves. They lived in their skin without concern for clothing. They slept under the stars amongst the chickens and the animals of the forest. Until that day I didn't even know they existed. But now that my eyes were opened, their world challenged my view of reality and I left my time in the forest changed.

You will be presented with opportunities to open yourself to the world in a new way. This is different from growth, because these experiences may not change who you are or what you do, anymore than the forest dwellers changed my wardrobe, or the meeting of the young couple in the temple changed Anna. Anna could continue in her life of prayer and fasting. I continued mine of clothing and work. The choice between familiarity and openness does not ask that you become the person you are talking with or move to the new town you discovered. It simply asks that you open your self to what God might be doing in places and people that are not a part of the familiar. It challenges you to open your eyes to this new reality. It asks you to be open to the unexpected.

One summer I traveled with a group of high school students to a town in Virginia. We had come to help out at a mission program in an inner city neighborhood there. The program worked with men and women who needed a second chance in their lives, many of them due to incarceration. The neighborhood saw people come and go from the prisons in what felt like an revolving door. Through the program, people could chose to take classes in the morning, then obtain job skills in the afternoon to help start a new life. We came to volunteer. The students worked hard that week. They painted houses. They worked in the second hand shop sorting clothing and donated items. They cleaned in the restaurant. But it wasn't the work that really mattered. It was the relationships. One day at a time, these young suburban students from Ohio got to know the people they were working with. These were two very different groups of people. There was nothing familiar for either group and finding common experiences to start from wasn't easy. At first the conversations felt awkward. What would the students from suburbs in Ohio and ex-offenders from Virginia talk about? But there seemed to be an unspoken commitment to openness. The conversations were guarded at first, carefully avoiding the obvious differences. Then one of the students and program members shared stories of their various scars from soccer injuries and street fights. They celebrated together about the upcoming fatherhood of one of the men and talked about baby clothes and parenting. The men of the program laughed and helped the students learn to paint properly and showed them around the neighborhood. The man who served as head chef in the local restaurant, a graduate of the program, made an amazing dinner complete with the best chocolate chip cookies in the world. By the end of the week it was like saying goodbye at summer camp. I watched as one of our students, a small blond haired junior girl, gave an enthusiastic hug goodbye to one of the men. He was well over six feet tall, with scars on his arm and a quiet, serious demeanor. But as they hugged he gave a small smile. In another corner of the room two of the teens laughed together with two other young men. A little girl from the neighborhood who spent time in the second hand shop had crawled up in the lap of another youth. The woman who owned one of the shops posed for pictures with the youth team that had worked with her. None of it was familiar. Neither group had changed to become anymore like the other. But on both sides the groups had chosen to be open to learn from one another. And our views of God's work in the lives of others had expanded.

What if you chose to intentionally keep your eyes open to new experiences? What if the very thing that God might want you to see today may be the same one that tempts you to shut your eyes? What if you avoided that temptation? What if, like Anna, you ran toward the unknown with openness, throwing aside the familiar, to see just what God might reveal? What would happen if you chose openness over familiarity?

Chapter 6
COURAGE OVER FEAR
Palmetto Bugs and Mountain Rescue

Orlando is a strange place to grow up. My parent's home was just thirty minutes from Disney World. Every winter our town was flooded with snow birds, looking to escape the cold from far off places I had only read about like Ohio and Wisconsin that had something they referred to as "snow." Each summer the snowbirds left and were replaced by families with sweaty children spending five years worth of savings to visit the theme parks. We knew attractions as the place where our friends worked when we were teenagers, and seasons were simply "hot" and "hotter." It was humid and crowded and full of mosquitos and palmetto bugs, which was a nice euphemism for giant roaches. But for me, it was home for 23 years. My family all lived there. I went to school in Florida all the way from preschool through college. On the same street where my friends and I kicked around a golf ball we also learned to ride a bike, then drive a car. My husband and I were married in a church just minutes from our parent's homes, which were one mile apart.

Two years after we were married, we were accepted to seminary. We opened our letters at the same time, and threw ourselves in to a hug with elation. We had prayed and planned for this next chapter in our lives, and now it would finally be a reality. Seminary would be the first step toward our dream of becoming pastors. There was just one small problem. Seminary was over one thousand miles from home, in a far off place called New Jersey.

We visited New Jersey just once before we moved. We loved the town where our graduate school was located, but we found New Jersey on the whole to be a very different kind of place than central Florida. We flew in to Newark in the dead of winter. February had taken its toll on the locals, who were bundled up in black pea coats and dark winter hats, their faces down to avoid the bitter wind that would cut right to your core. We exited our plane still glowing from the Florida sun, clad in brightly colored ski jackets, and began trying to strike up conversations on the NJ transit. We found quickly that New Jersey meant more snow, less sweet tea and sunshine, and people who do not simply strike up a conversation on the commuter train.

Setting aside our concerns about the inevitable culture shock, we began making plans to move to New Jersey for school that fall. As the boxes began multiplying in our small apartment living room, I felt a deep sense of unease growing in the pit of my stomach. I couldn't put words on it, but the sensation began to grow from a small troubling feeling to a monster of anxiety that demanded my attention. As the weeks went on, just looking at the packed boxes made my heart rate quicken and my breathing grow shallow. At the time, I didn't realize how deeply my roots went in Florida. I knew I had grown up there, but I didn't realize how much of my identity and sense of self I had invested in this southern community. But my spirit must have begun to spin about my impeding relocation, because within a matter of weeks the unease blew up into full panic attacks, something I had not experienced before.

We loaded the U-haul, and I watched our familiar town fly past the windows as I munched on cheese crackers and nervously sipped a diet soda. We crossed the state line and I tried to control my breathing as we began the trek north to our new home. After we arrived, my spirit calmed down for a few days with the distraction of settling in to our apartment, but soon the anxiety returned with a vengeance, with an alter ego I came to know as depression. I had never experienced feelings like these. I had experienced worry or sadness, but never emotions so strong that I felt so unlike myself. I looked over pictures from my life in Florida and wondered what had happened to that happy girl in the photos. She seemed so carefree, so unlike this young woman who felt trapped by her feelings. Things that had once been easy, a trip to the grocery store or writing a paper, took all of my energy and left me exhausted.

I soon began the work of therapy. My struggles became a catalyst for growth over the next several years of fighting toward a new sense of self. The anxiety proved easier to control than the depression for me, but neither were going to be subdued without a fight. Every person who battles these monsters must chose their own path to healing. For some, it is medication. For others, exercise or talk therapy. For me, I found my way through a combination of talk therapy and acupuncture and lots of prayer.

As a part of the battle, I quickly found others who were having to find their strength as well. I found that most do not wear their struggles as a badge, but disguise them under a facade of calm, and may only share with others who struggle too. No matter which path they took to healing, one thing was common amongst us all. Healing took courage, courage we didn't know we had. Depression and anxiety want those who fight them to believe the lie that they are weak, that they should be afraid. Depression would tell me I couldn't possibly face the day. Anxiety wanted me to believe I would never feel strong again. But they were lies. Each day was difficult, and courage was the only choice to move ahead.

I wish I could say that progress was a straight forward line from struggle to strength, but it wasn't. Some days were good. I felt strong and like myself again. Other days I would feel like I was back in the hole, alone. But courage pulled me, one day at a time, on the upward path toward wholeness. The kind of courage that comes only from God.

At some point in each of our lives, we find ourselves in front of a situation that seems terrifying or impossible. Fear releases adrenaline through our body. Our eyes widen and our heart pounds. Our palms sweat and our knees shake. We are facing a relocation to a new town, and the stacks of boxes terrify us with the reality of a new life. The stick shows a faint line, an unplanned pregnancy, and we realize in an instant our life has been turned upside down. The doctor calls with test results and as she begins to discuss treatment options, fear of an unknown future clouds our minds and her voice fades. We are asked to speak at a conference, and as we walk on to the platform and see the sea of faces our body tells us to run as if the people there were a pack of wolves.

Rahab's life was not the one she had planned for or desired. She had made her living as a prostitute. The other women in the town wouldn't be seen with her. The men looked at her as a commodity. The days and nights blurred together and she dreamt of a way out. But what else could she do? How would she put food on her table? One evening she heard a frantic knock on her door:

> Then Joshua son of Nun sent two men secretly from Shittim as spies, saying, 'Go, view the land, especially Jericho.' So they went, and entered the house of a prostitute whose name was Rahab, and spent the night there. The king of Jericho was told, 'Some Israelites have come here tonight to search out the land.' Then the king of Jericho sent orders to Rahab, 'Bring out the men who have come to you, who entered your house, for they have come only to search out the whole land.' (Joshua 2:1-3, NRSV)

Rahab was a tough woman. She had seen a lot in her life and was not easily frightened. But this was a strange turn of events. Spies knocking on her door looking for a place to hide. The king himself finds out and sends her an order to reveal them. Rahab knows that these men are there on God's purposes. The power of the king is real, and she has every reason to be afraid. Rahab, however, chooses courage over fear.

> But the woman took the two men and hid them. Then she said, 'True, the men came to me, but I did not know where they came from. And when it

was time to close the gate at dark, the men went out. Where the men went I do not know. Pursue them quickly, for you can overtake them.' She had, however, brought them up to the roof and hidden them with the stalks of flax that she had laid out on the roof. So the men pursued them on the way to the Jordan as far as the fords. As soon as the pursuers had gone out, the gate was shut. (Joshua 2:4-7, NRSV)

Rahab sends the king's men on a fools errand. She hides the spies on her rooftop and sends the scouts away on a false trail. The punishment for lying to the king's men would be swift and serious, especially for a woman, a prostitute no less, who held no power in the community. But she does not waver in her bravery. Once she is sure the scouts are gone, she returns to the spies.

Before they went to sleep, she came up to them on the roof and said to the men: 'I know that the Lord has given you the land, and that dread of you has fallen on us, and that all the inhabitants of the land melt in fear before you. For we have heard how the Lord dried up the water of the Red Sea before you when you came out of Egypt, and what you did to the two kings of the Amorites that were beyond the Jordan, to Sihon and Og, whom you utterly destroyed. As soon as we heard it, our hearts failed, and there was no courage left in any of us because of you. The Lord your God is indeed God in heaven above and on earth below. Now then, since I have dealt kindly with you, swear to me by the Lord that you in turn will deal kindly with my family. Give me a sign of good faith that you will spare my father and mother, my brothers and sisters, and all who belong to them, and deliver our lives from death.' The men said to her, 'Our life for yours! If you do not tell this business of ours, then we will deal kindly and faithfully with you when the Lord gives us the land.' Then she let them down by a rope through the window, for her house was on the outer side of the city wall and she resided within the wall itself. She said to them, 'Go towards the hill country, so that the pursuers may not come upon you. Hide yourselves there for three days, until the pursuers have returned; then afterwards you may go on your way.' (Joshua 2:8-16, NRSV)

Rahab again chooses courage. She approaches the spies and strikes a deal to ensure the safety of her family in the battles ahead. Rahab could have given in to fear. When the spies knocked at her door, she could have sent them away. The king's men came demanding information and she could have surrendered the spies. Once the scouts had departed, she could have sent the men away without first asking for protection for her family. In each moment, Rahab has every reason to be afraid. These decisions could cost her her life. She is faced with a choice. Each time, she chooses courage over fear.

You have the same choice. You will be faced with those situations that threaten to overtake you with fear. Fear serves a healthy function. It keeps us from taking risks that could threaten our lives. It identifies danger. If you stumble upon a bear on a hiking trail, fear is a healthy response. The adrenaline gives our bodies the strength to defend ourselves against the animal. In my case, when faced with a bear, fear gives my feet the energy to run for the hills.

But there is no bear. There are, however, situations for each of us that make our knees quake. Sometimes these are the opportunities to take risks and follow God in to difficult places. The life God calls you to is full of twists and turns. These twists may make a bear on a hiking trail seem like a welcome alternative. At each of these moments, God presents you with a choice. Will you give in to fear, choosing the easier path? Or will you, like Rahab, chose courage? These moments may be the ones that define our lives. Until that moment, Rahab's life was not the one she had dreamed of. She had hardened herself to a world that was unkind and unjust. Then a knock came at her door. She chose to embrace the opportunity before her. Now Rahab was an essential figure in the drama of God's work with Israel. It wasn't easy. But Rahab chose to serve the God who makes us brave.

The good news is that we don't face this path alone. Those men and women who came alongside of me as I navigated my way toward emotional health served as guides. Their courage helped me find my own. If they could find their way through the hardest hours, then I knew I could too. If you are currently facing a fear in your life, seek out these people. Not the ones who will enable your fear and encourage you to give up. Seek out those in your life who have developed the courage to face the life God calls them in to, and walk alongside of them.

Perhaps you have faced fear and come out on the other side. You find yourself in a time of calm. Open your life to walk with others who need your strength. Your story may not be an easy one to tell. But there are people God will intersect with your life who are looking for someone who has conquered the obstacles they face. You can be their guide. You chose courage. They need you to show them the way.

We need one another as we chose courage over fear. A group of three teenage girls from the youth group at my church went hiking in the mountains one afternoon. Wanting a challenge, they took the trail known to be the most difficult. From the first few steps in to the woods the incline increased dramatically, and they steadied themselves with the branches hanging overhead. One step at a time they went deeper in to the forest and farther up the mountain, keeping a brisk pace as they climbed. Twenty minutes in to the hike, one of the girls sank to the ground. She was dehydrated and confused. She was too ill to retrace their steps back down the path. The girls sat on either side of their friend and quickly dialed the number for my cell phone. Their voices were calm but shaky and they told me what had happened. As I hung up the phone, the teenagers sitting with me looked concerned. I gathered my things and told them I needed to go to the trail with one of our other leaders to hike up to the girls while we waited for medical help to arrive. Without hesitating, the teens jumped up. "We're coming with you."

We piled in to my SUV and headed to the trail head, calling the paramedics along the way as the girl's condition deteriorated. The girls had called again and she wasn't responding to them. As soon as we reached the first turn in the trail, a large group of dark clouds moved across the blue sky and thunder rumbled in the distance. We continued farther in to the woods and the thunder grew louder until the ground shook. Lightening flashed through the trees and the rain started in earnest. Within seconds we were soaked from head to toe. The clay of the trail began to dissolve in to the rain and formed a small slippery river at our feet. Even the paramedics were having trouble making it up the incline. After several minutes of slipping and climbing, holding on tightly to the trees around us, our group made it to the top. One of the teens brought a blanket, and they held it over their friend to shelter her from the storm. The others gathered around, offering silent prayers and support as the medics began their work. The storm continued to pound through the forest but despite constant encouragement that they should return to the car, the teens wouldn't budge. Their friend needed them.

There was plenty of room for fear. But what I saw that afternoon in the eyes of those students was courage. The two friends sat bravely on either side of the girl, refusing to leave her alone. The rest of the teens hiking up the mountain in a gigantic storm, determined to help their friend. The teens carried equipment for paramedics, navigated a treacherous mountain trail, and then insisted on following the ambulance to the hospital to wait for her release. They huddled together in the emergency room, shivering as the cool air inside the building met their drenched clothing. After an hour they received word that she was fine, and huge smiles broke out on their faces. They later laughed and called themselves "mountain rescue." I call them people of courage. The courage that God gave to each of them that day sustained their friend in her time of fear. They chose to be brave so that she could be too.

Is there something in your life you are afraid of facing? What would it look like to seek out courage to face whatever lies ahead? Is there something you have lived through that was difficult? How can you use that experience to encourage others to be brave?

Chapter 7
PEOPLE OVER PRODUCTIVITY
Pajama Party with Strangers

Long before we were married or went to seminary, before there were kids or a mortgage or groceries to buy, my husband and I would sit in coffee shops and dream of trips we would take some day. Our wanderlust was a unifying force between us, and we would stare at maps for hours making plans of the trips we would take. One evening we went so far as to draw out a route across the country on an atlas of the United States. The route crossed over mountains and went through national parks. It connected major cities and highways that ran through long stretches of open road. The line just went one direction, from east to west, and I am not sure how we planned on getting home. Despite its lack of practicality, the map felt like a contract between the two of us, that the dreams we had would one day be realized. Eventually the atlas was packed in a trunk and mostly forgotten for years, as we scraped our way through graduate school together, had our two children and lived through the early parenting years of sleep deprivation and potty training. Taking a trip came in second to preschool orientations, house hunting and settling in to our jobs. Years later, when our children were in their later grades of elementary school, the church where I served offered me a summer sabbatical. Three months of paid leave was given to experience growth and time for reflection before starting the next phase of ministry. Three months of time off was something I hadn't experienced since high school. What would I do with this gift of time? The map my husband and I had drawn over a decade ago seemed to whisper to us from the trunk where it was packed away. The dreams of our youth forced their way back in to our consciousness. The time had come.

We pulled out the map and put it in to a frame, and began to draw potential routes on the glass using dry erase markers. The original plan needed adjusting, as it originated in Florida instead of where we currently lived in Ohio, and did not have a way to return home. After many nights of dreaming and planning the black line showing our route was set: almost 10,000 miles, as far east as New York City, as far north as Montreal, then all the way out west to Seattle, south to LA and then back east to Ohio. It was ambitious and slightly crazy, but we were committed. As with all good planning, the next step for me, the child of two computer programmers, was obvious. I would create a spreadsheet. I began devising an in-depth document to handle the details of our six week adventure with our two children. As we planned, we realized that while our teenage selves may have been fine sleeping in the car, our family of four would need actual lodging. We booked a few campgrounds and started looking at hotels, suddenly realizing how much this adventure might cost. Studying the map and comparing it with our social media, we began to find friends from graduate school that lived all across the country. I contacted them asking for a square of carpet to crash on for a night on our way. When our contacts ran out, I got braver and started emailing churches to ask for a place to camp in their building. Soon the empty column of "lodging" on the spreadsheet starting filling up with the homes of friends and family. Other rows listed the names of church buildings that were willing to let us sleep in their library. As the trip drew nearer the list included names of people we had not seen since we slept as children on their living room floor in sleeping bags, and even names of strangers who had offered us their hospitality. I knew as we packed our car that this was outside my comfort zone to show up on the doorstep of someone I had never met and stay for the night. For me, meeting with strangers was something I did in reception lines at church wearing a suit not in their homes in my pajamas. But the map and the teenagers that drew it silenced my adult hesitations, and we set off with our cots, a tent, and a spreadsheet stored safely in the glove compartment.

We knew in planning the trip that the things we would do and see would be amazing. The Badlands were more beautiful that we could have imagined, the layers of colored rock taking our breath away. We hiked through the Redwood forest with its majestic trees towering over us, their tops disappearing in to the sky. Our children were delighted by the street performers of San Francisco, and they still talk about a croissant they had at a Farmer's Market in Vermont. But as we traveled, we were surprised by how it was not so much the sights we saw or the things we did that were affecting us. The people we encountered along the way began to take a leading role in the story of our travels. In Montreal we had emailed a church to see if we could stay in their building. The pastor and his wife responded and invited us to stay with them in their home. Weeks later we would stand on their doorstep in a quaint courtyard in this unfamiliar city. As we knocked on the door to their home I wondered what we were thinking. What would it be like to stay in the home of someone we had never met? Several hours later I realized these people we considered strangers were now friends. We shared about our lives on the couches of their living room. We heard about life in a town much different from our own, and left our time there renewed. We continued on the trip and friends we had not seen in almost ten years since graduate school welcomed us with open arms in to their lives, sharing dinner with us around their dining tables. Our trip album is full of pictures not only of places, but of people who made our six week trip possible. By the end of our traveling, we found a certain loneliness in the stops without these people who defined the trip in a way the spreadsheet could never have predicted. People, it turns out, were what the trip was about far more than what we accomplished along the way.

This is easy for us to forget. We live in a world that values productivity above relationship. We see this in our lengthy to-do lists and efficiency seminars. It creeps in to our interactions when we ask our spouse "what did you do today? instead of "how are you?" We pride ourselves on busy schedules and post photos of our accomplishments. Our sense of self becomes intricately connected with what we can check off a list. Productivity shows us we are contributing to society. It proves that we have worth. It demonstrates our abilities and strengths. It begins to define who we are.

Martha certainly understood the value of hard work. When Martha heard that Jesus was coming, she set off in to a flurry of activity. The floor needed to be swept. The table should be cleared off. Her mind raced trying to pull together a meal from the various vegetables that were ready in the garden. Her hands moved hurriedly from one task to another and before she could finish she heard Jesus' footsteps approach. Martha rushed to the door and welcomed him warmly in to her home. Knowing there was still more to do, she showed him a comfortable place to sit then returned to her whirlwind of hospitality preparations. After a few minutes, her sister Mary joined them. Mary always carried an air about her of calm. Martha was the sister who was always busy. There was always another chore that could be done. There was always another meal to prepare. It wasn't that Martha didn't love her sister. But she just couldn't see somedays how they could even be related. While Martha could point to a list of accomplishments at the end of a day, Mary appeared to float from thing to the next, seemingly unconcerned with how much she could complete. This particular afternoon Mary's lackadaisical nature frustrated Martha. She felt her anger grow as Mary glided in to the room, and then positioned herself sitting next to Jesus to listen to what he was saying. Martha's exasperation is apparent when she even shares with Jesus her criticism of her sister.

> Now as they went on their way, he entered a certain village, where a woman named Martha welcomed him into her home. She had a sister named Mary, who sat at the Lord's feet and listened to what he was saying. But Martha was distracted by her many tasks; so she came to him and asked, "Lord, do you not care that my sister has left me to do all the work by myself? Tell her then to help me." (Luke 10:38-40, NRSV)

I find myself sympathizing with Martha in this moment. We are sometimes given only a few minutes notice to someone coming to visit our home, and I am not a stranger to the flurry of shoving things under the couch, throwing dishes in to the sink and desperately searching the pantry for food to offer the unexpected company. No doubt her activity came from a well intentioned desire to be a hospitable host. This was not just any guest. This was Jesus. Martha knew what was being said about him, about who he was. She had heard the stories about him in the streets. Then here he was, the man she had heard so much about, coming to her home. It was essential that she give him the welcome he deserved.

But Jesus has another take on Martha's frantic work:

> But the Lord answered her, "Martha, Martha, you are worried and distracted by many things; there is need of only one thing. Mary has chosen the better part, which will not be taken away from her." (Luke 10:41-42, NRSV)

Notice that Jesus does not offer Martha a word of correction until he is specifically asked. He knew her heart, that she did these things as an act of hospitality for him. She knew it wasn't her intention to ignore Jesus, but in fact quite the opposite. There seems to be a pastoral, loving tone in his words. With a bemused look in his eye, he gently redirects her attention. Mary is not choosing to be lazy. Mary has seen past the dust on the floor and the lack of food gracing their table to the person sitting before her. Hospitality was of utmost importance. But what hospitality meant in that moment was different than what Martha believed. The thing that needed to be done could not be checked off a list. It wouldn't take any tools. What needed to be done was to put the person in front of her on top of the list, to make room in her life for him. This person was Jesus.

We have a sense of what needs to be done each day. For some, it is a list kept in your mind or on a phone. For others, it is noticing what is unfinished at home or at work. We move through this list, feeling a sense of satisfaction at the completion of a task. Lists keep us focused and help us not forget what must be done. Productivity, in and of itself, is not to be abandoned entirely. In Mary and Martha's case, someone would need to keep the house, prepare the meals, provide for their family. It is not the acts themselves that are to blame.

The problem comes when our lists and the people around us collide. The people in our lives cannot always be neatly fit in to a box to be checked off. The needs of the people around us are not always predictable or scheduled. A spouse gets sick. A coworker has a new idea. A friend stops by unexpectedly. A child wants to share about their day at school. These are not things we can point to at the end of the day that we have accomplished. They are usually not on a list, or blocked in to our schedule. The people in our lives show up unexpectedly. They become interruptions.

Many of us have heard it said before that God often is most present in just such an interruption. It is in these moments that we see God at work the most clearly, in ways we could never have anticipated. But why? Because God is at work through people, not productivity. We experience God's voice and presence through one another. God shows up in the conversation we have with our son who had a difficult day at school. God works through the idea of our coworker as we listen. God uses us as we support our spouse in their illness. Experiencing the presence of Jesus Christ by sitting at his feet as a disciple was not on the list for the day. But it was exactly where the women needed to be.

To call these moment interruptions is to honor that there are things that need to be done. We don't need to sit by the window simply waiting for someone to come by. It is not God's purpose that we spiritualize the role of coach potato under the guise of waiting for God's people to come to our door. It is in the daily business we attend to that we open the opportunity to encounter people. In an amusing irony, we have to be actively engaged in our work to chose to abandon it.

 I wrote these sentences while sitting in the quiet of my living room on my laptop. As I finished typing, my phone rang. It was our office administrator at the church, calling to share a story. Our church office is always a flurry of activity. There are always multiple things to be done, and our administrator is on the frontline of a constantly ringing phone and revolving door of appointments. A company who donates baked items to our church for those in need had made their regular food delivery that morning. Before calling to have them picked up by the appropriate volunteers, she thought of inviting the teenagers with whom we work to stop by and share a pastry and some conversation. Some of these teens have true hardship in their lives, both emotionally and financially, and this would offer a chance to connect over a baked good. She knew her to-do list was beckoning her, but this seemed like too good of an opportunity to be missed. Within a few minutes, one of the teens arrived with his two brothers. The teen, a high school student, regularly helps his mother by offering to take care of his brothers when he is able. This was the first time he had brought them to the church, and the administrator was able to meet them and watch him as he cared for his brothers. She noticed the gentle way he guided his much younger siblings, with leadership far beyond his years. They sat and talked together for the remainder of the hour until he left to take them home. She had a million things to do that day. She could have easily just sent the baked donations on to their final destination with an email and returned to her work. She didn't. She chose the interruption. And God was there.

You will be faced with this choice almost everyday. You will be presented with the opportunity to chose between people and productivity. Productivity carries a significant temptation. If you stop and attend to the person in front of you, you may not get through everything on your list. You may not be able to accomplish what you set out to do that day. But what is the worst that can happen if your list sits unfinished? What if the interruption is what you were supposed to do today? What if the person in front of you is God's appointment for you? How would you treat this person differently if this were Jesus?

Chapter 8
GROWTH OVER STAGNATION
My Father the Alligator

My father and I would often go exploring on Saturdays when I was young, finding adventures around every corner in our town. Sometimes our trips would take us in to bowling alleys or pool halls. One spring we spent an entire week sampling every putt putt golf course within a fifty mile radius. Other times we would eat fast food tacos way too close to dinner time with the promise of consuming green beans and meatloaf at home to hide our treachery. When the weather wasn't too hot, we would drive the familiar winding road to the springs to go canoeing. The river there was relatively small and manageable for a father and his young daughter to navigate. The trees hung slightly over the water, providing relief from the intense Florida sun, and on a good day the breeze that made the hanging moss sway hypnotically also kept the mosquitoes at bay. We would paddle quietly around the bends in the waterway, our oars rippling the glassy surface, watching the tiny fish dart in and out of the reeds and the occasional turtle sunning itself on a log.

This being Florida the waterway was also the home to alligators, although I had never seen one. I had learned from a young age to keep a close eye out, especially in the stiller waters, where an alligator could be resting, camouflaged as a floating log. The alligators were not especially dangerous unless you happened to run your canoe in to one, which would be easy to do in the narrow winding waterway through the woods.

My father, with whom life is never dull, had perfected his alligator imitation. His favorite pastime as we paddled along would be to wait until the water was still and the forest was quiet. He would then let out a slow, low croak from the back of the canoe. By the third or fourth "alligator", I was wise to his antics and no longer swiveled my head nervously at the sound. This particular day we had glided gently in to a large pond area of the springs. The water was so still you could see the insects skittering across the top, the surface tension unbroken. I sat peacefully in the front of our canoe, scanning the shoreline for turtles. Then, from behind me I heard again a low, loud croaking sound erupt above the hum of the crickets. "Very funny dad" I muttered, still looking ahead but smiling at his attempt to trick me. But as I turned and looked back at him my smile faded when I saw the seriousness in his face. "That one wasn't me, " he said quietly. We plunged our oars into the water and stroked quickly in unison without looking back to see if the alligator had surfaced again.

We learned that afternoon that still water is to be eyed with suspicion. It can harbor alligators among the water reeds. It can also hide shallow depths that are dangerous for diving. It can house bacteria that causes illness. Stagnate water can be dangerous. Stagnation in our lives is dangerous too. We become comfortable in our daily lives and begin to avoid things that might challenge us. We set aside dreams deeming them too big. We decide it is too late to change who we are and settle for our current state. We chose stagnation over growth as the apparent safer choice, but in fact put ourselves in the most likely place to find an alligator.

Deborah was a woman who chose growth at every opportunity. She held a position highly unusual for a woman in her time, called by God not only as a prophetess but a judge. She could have at any time chosen comfort, deeming the path ahead too difficult. She could have pushed aside God's call in her life, deciding it was a dream that was just too outlandish to be possible. She could have blamed her position as a woman on her avoidance of the opportunities before her. She could have easily chosen stagnation. Her story, however, could not be more different:

> The Israelites again did what was evil in the sight of the Lord, after Ehud died. So the Lord sold them into the hand of King Jabin of Canaan, who reigned in Hazor; the commander of his army was Sisera, who lived in Harosheth-ha-goiim. Then the Israelites cried out to the Lord for help; for he had nine hundred chariots of iron, and had oppressed the Israelites cruelly for twenty years. At that time Deborah, a prophetess, wife of Lappidoth, was judging Israel. She used to sit under the palm of Deborah between Ramah and Bethel in the hill country of Ephraim; and the Israelites came up to her for judgement. She sent and summoned Barak son of Abinoam from Kedesh in Naphtali, and said to him, 'The Lord, the God of Israel, commands you, "Go, take position at Mount Tabor, bringing ten thousand from the tribe of Naphtali and the tribe of Zebulun. I will draw out Sisera, the general of Jabin's army, to meet you by the Wadi Kishon with his chariots and his troops; and I will give him into your hand." ' Barak said to her, 'If you will go with me, I will go; but if you will not go with me, I will not go.' And she said, 'I will surely go with you; nevertheless, the road on which you are going will not lead to your glory, for the Lord will sell Sisera into the hand of a woman.'

Then Deborah got up and went with Barak to Kedesh. Barak summoned Zebulun and Naphtali to Kedesh; and ten thousand warriors went up behind him; and Deborah went up with him. Now Heber the Kenite had separated from the other Kenites, that is, the descendants of Hobab the father-in-law of Moses, and had encamped as far away as Elon-bezaanannim, which is near Kedesh. When Sisera was told that Barak son of Abinoam had gone up to Mount Tabor, Sisera called out all his chariots, nine hundred chariots of iron, and all the troops who were with him, from Harosheth-ha-goiim to the Wadi Kishon. Then Deborah said to Barak, 'Up! For this is the day on which the Lord has given Sisera into your hand. The Lord is indeed going out before you.' So Barak went down from Mount Tabor with ten thousand warriors following him. And the Lord threw Sisera and all his chariots and all his army into a panic before Barak; Sisera got down from his chariot and fled away on foot, while Barak pursued the chariots and the army to Harosheth-ha-goiim. All the army of Sisera fell by the sword; no one was left. (Judges 4:1-16, NRSV)

Here, the center of the Old Testament, we find the story of a woman who has not let any obstacle keep her from continuing to grow. As a prophetess and then a judge, she was already a leader for her people. But instead of letting that be enough, she prophesies the freedom of the people of Israel, her people, from their oppressor. Then she accompanies the troops in to battle and sees her prophesy from God realized as a warrior among the men fighting for freedom.

Overachiever.

Admittedly there is something about Deborah that seems a little out of reach, a bit unrealistic for many of us. We celebrate that her testimony is there, especially as a woman. We stand in awe of her ability to be a prophetess, receiving God's vision for the people, a direct line between her people and her God. We applaud her role as a judge, navigating the disagreements of the Israelites as they lived in community together. We are impressed by her bravery to serve also as a warrior, leading the troops in to battle against an army with "nine hundred chariots of iron." We cheer as her armies are victorious and their oppressor is overthrown. But there is something that may leave us a little frustrated by this story. How can we live up to someone who can predict the future, bring harmony to the people, and lead her troops in to battle when we went out today with our shirt on inside out? Is a story like Deborah's the kind that paralyzes us in our stagnation instead of encouraging us to growth due to the scope of her achievements?

What if we take a step back. The story does an excellent job at portraying the faithfulness and bravery of this woman who continued to move forward in her life, never choosing comfort or laziness over the gentle nudge, or sometimes push, of God. What it doesn't share is the seemingly insurmountable obstacles she may have felt, the difficult choices she had to make along the way. Perhaps Deborah experienced, as many of us do, feelings of inadequacy or fear. She may have worried about her advice to the latest people to visit with her as a judge who still seemed to be at odds. She may have wondered if she had really heard the prophecy correctly that they should fight their oppressor. As she prepared for battle, she may have dwelled on the risks to her life and the soldiers who fought with her. She may have even considered turning them all around and going home.

We don't know what hesitations Deborah faced. What we do know is that any obstacles she had, any temptation she had to retreat in to seemingly safer still water, she pushed aside in her desire to follow God. She willingly chose to embrace the plans God had for her life, even though there were so many paths that would have been easier for her to take. Deborah chose growth in her life. She chose God. And in doing so she left the seemingly innocuous still waters that could have drowned her in stagnation for the rushing, dangerous but exciting waters of growth.

Stagnation in your life carries that same risk of drowning that Deborah faced. God will put opportunities before you to grow in your character, your abilities, your relationships, your faith. These opportunities will often seem as crazy as riding a canoe over the edge of Niagara Falls. The calmer life you currently inhabit will seem safer, more secure. But what would happen if you chose to believe that you could grow, as Deborah grew, one step at a time, following in God's path? Have you sensed an opportunity to follow God in to uncharted territory, but have let obstacles of insecurity or fear get in your way? Have you felt like you were too old or too shy or too busy to step out and do something you sensed a leading to do? Have you become so comfortable in stagnation that you have lost sight of what these new opportunities might look like? You start this movement toward growth not all at once, but by taking one step. The story of Deborah didn't all unfold in one day. There were periods of the mundane. There were days when nothing extraordinary happened, and she went about her day that seemed identical to the day before. There were senseless squabbles to negotiate with her people. There were days when she sat ready to receive them as a judge and no one came. The prophecies were fantastic when they were given, but there were many days when she received no word from the Lord for her people. Some days the Israelites would cry out for guidance, for a glimpse of what God had in store. She would search her heart for that still small voice, and find only silence. When we look at the story in just a few paragraphs, we lose sight of the slow, daily progress on the path God had for her, and see only the exciting achievements, listed one after the other in apparent quick succession.

Growth takes time. As you intentionally chose growth over stagnation, the movement may be almost imperceivable in the day to day of your life. Some days it will seem like nothing has really changed, that your boat is sitting unmoved in the still pond among the reeds. Some days will be extraordinary. On these days you will see huge progress in the direction God is leading you. The waters will rush and roar, and you will feel the thrill of God at work in your life as you grow and change.

Sharon had felt the waters gently moving for quite a while. She had felt a small push for years to volunteer in a homeless shelter. But there was always an obstacle. Her children needed her, then her grandchildren. There were meals to fix and soccer games to attend. Her days were full of appointments and other volunteering. There were lots of reasons to stay docked in the still water, right where she was. She was already helping in the community in other ways. Yet still the nudge continued. After a change in her family situation, the spirit of God moved again, and she couldn't ignore it any longer. Despite the obstacles, despite her hesitations, she knew she must respond. Sharon chose growth. That afternoon she looked at her schedule and made some choices to free up her time. Then she took a deep breath and made a call to the shelter's volunteer department. She still had questions and hesitations. She knew there would be situations for which she wasn't prepared. She questioned her own ability to serve in this different way. After all of these years, well in to her retirement, would she really be able to start something so new? But the waters were moving now. It was time for Sharon to take the next steps to grow in a new direction, right where God was leading her to be. Stagnation would have kept her where she was comfortable, doing what she already knew. But God called her to grow.

What would you do if you trusted God and took a new direction in your life? What would be a first step for you? Could you listen to your life and to God and see where new opportunities might be forming? Is there an opportunity for growth you have been avoiding? What would it look like to, despite the obstacles, chose growth over stagnation?

Chapter 9
PURPOSE OVER PLANS
Nativity Warfare

Christmas was going to be extra special this year. My two sons were finally both at the age to really appreciate all of the trimmings and trappings. The snow had blanketed our town with a sparkling white cover that made even the crowded parking lots look magical. In our living room stood the Christmas tree we had tromped through the snow to cut down. We had wandered from one tree to the next, grading each on its height and fullness, until finally settling on our selection, which was slightly lopsided but rose above the others in the field, our star just touching the ceiling when it was erected inside. Several shiny packages sat enticingly arranged beneath its branches, the lights twinkling beneath macaroni noodle ornaments and delicate glass globes. Two fabulously tacky gingerbread houses graced the center of our table, covered from top to bottom in marshmallows and gum drops, with the exception of a few bare spots where candy had been stealthily removed and gobbled up when I was not looking.

I could see the magic of Christmas glittering in the eyes of my two sons. I knew this would be the year that we would not only make Christmas cookies and drink hot cocoa by the fire. This would also be the year we would talk to them about the meaning of Christmas, the story of the birth of Jesus Christ in the manger so many years ago. We had read books about it with them from the time they were still in a crib, but I wanted them to truly experience the wonder of the story that was so essential to our faith. One afternoon while out shopping, I came across a nativity set that was just perfect. It had just enough pieces that I knew it would interest them both, but was tough enough to withstand two young boys handling it, unlike the crystal ones on the higher shelves at the store. It had animals the characters could ride and a small cardboard barn to house the holy family. I sat holding it in the store and began playing the scene out in my mind.

I would bring home the perfectly age appropriate nativity set and put it together with the boys. My three year old would open his eyes wide in fascination, with an innate sense of the holiness of this special toy. He would gingerly pick up one piece at a time and place them in their appropriate spots in the scene, then quietly act out the birth narrative from the gospel of Luke, all the while humming Silent Night with glimmers of faith stirring in his heart while I made Christmas cookies in the kitchen.

I drove home feeling satisfied and, admittedly, proud of my parenting decision. This was not another toy to put under the tree. This would be an instrument to explore faith together. I turned the corner onto our snow covered street and pulled excitedly in to our driveway. As if he knew, my three year old greeted me at the door with an eager hug, ready to play. I could already hear the opening bars of Silent Night starting in my head. I led him quietly over to the coffee table and slowly revealed the box from within the store bag. I could see his hands fidgeting at his side with anticipation, but he listened carefully to me as I explained the toy, all the while keeping one eye on the box. I explained slowly that this was not just any toy, but a very special God toy. I let my voice take on a serious hush to impart the mystery and importance of this moment. I shared that this would help us understand the birth of Jesus, and that we play with it in a different way than other toys. I continued in a lengthy explanation of the purpose of this toy, and my three year old waited with the most patience he could muster. I set the pieces out softly on the rug, and stole away to the kitchen with a triumphant smile on my face. It was all working out according to plan. I began gathering the ingredients for the Christmas cookies that would complete the scene when I heard muffled noises from the other room. I paused to listen for what I was sure would be my son now interacting with the Christmas story. Maybe he was pretending to be a sheep, or making noises for the baby Jesus. Or maybe he was pretending to be a shepherd or a wise man or an angel. But the noise sounded different, and I tip toed closer to the living room to peek in at him.

He was still playing with the nativity set, as I had left him, and his eyes were shining with happiness. But there were some foreign characters in the scene now. I recognized several storm troopers from his toy box wielding large laser guns and light sabers. I watched with wide eyes as he made the appropriate noises for their weapons and took out an open assault on the holy family. Joseph fell to the blow of a light saber, the angel flew from the laser gun and the cradle tipped over in the chaos. Sheep were knocked over one by one like dominoes, and the wise men now formed an army of resistance against the intrusion. Instead of the Christmas story this was now an open battle scene. My son continued, making the "pwu! pwu! pwu!" of the lasers as I walked slowly back in to the kitchen, the theme from Star Wars now taking the place of Silent Night in my subconscious.

We make plans. We make plans for our children and their development. We picture the scene in our mind and imagine how things will unfold. We make plans for our week and what we will do or accomplish. We plan what we will eat or what we will wear. We plan what we will do for a career, or where we will travel next summer. Some of our plans are haphazardly thrown together and quickly set aside when they don't come to fruition. Others are painstakingly drawn out, one detail at a time, and we are devastated when we are thrown off course.

Esther had plans for her life like anyone else. Her journey had not been easy. Esther was an orphan, for both of her parents had died when she was young. A man named Mordecai had graciously taken her in, and from there her life had continued. Life still wasn't easy, but she had a home and food to eat. As a woman in the kingdom, she had heard stories filtering through the people of what was happening in the palace. The women whispered that the Queen, Vashti, had not obeyed the king and that he was displeased. She heard that there was a new decree to gather the women together who were not married and bring them to the palace.

Esther's plans are no longer her own. With the other women she is gathered in to the palace grounds and put through a series of treatments and advice like something out of a bizarre dating game show. Her beauty does not go unnoticed, and she is soon a leading contender to be queen. Ester takes her place in the palace. It was nothing she could ever have planned for or imagined. Just a year ago she was living a quiet life with Mordecai, and now she lived as royalty. The other women had looked at her with jealousy as she was selected for this new life. But Esther had not forgotten what had happened to Vashti at the hands of the king.

Esther must have wondered why her life had taken this turn. Just as she settles in to this new life, her life change again. Esther receives word from Mordecai that there are plans to assassinate the king, and she runs to tell him, earning his appreciation. She has saved the life of the king. Just when Esther's life quiets down again, she receives another batch of unsettling news. As she receives the report, her heart stops and her eyes widen. Mordecai had refused to bow down before the king. Because he is a Jew, an advisor to the king has advised that all of the Jews be put to death. Esther's mind races. Mordecai. Her friends. What will happen to them? And what will happen when the king learns that his new queen, the one who saved his life, is one of the very people he has now decreed must die?

Esther paces back and forth in her room in the palace, each plan she contrives seeming as crazy as the last. She corresponds with Moredecai. She knows in the end she must approach the king. She is their only hope. But she had heard the stories of Vashti, she knows the laws and what is at stake. To approach the king could means her death. As they correspond, God's purposes begin to unfold:

> Then Esther spoke to Hathach and gave him a message for Mordecai, saying, 'All the king's servants and the people of the king's provinces know that if any man or woman goes to the king inside the inner court without being called, there is but one law—all alike are to be put to death. Only if the king holds out the golden scepter to someone, may that person live. I myself have not been called to come in to the king for thirty days.' When they told Mordecai what Esther had said, Mordecai told them to reply to Esther, 'Do not think that in the king's palace you will escape any more than all the other Jews. For if you keep silence at such a time as this, relief and deliverance will rise for the Jews from another quarter, but you and your father's family will perish. Who knows? Perhaps you have come to royal dignity for just such a time as this.' Then Esther said in reply to Mordecai, 'Go, gather all the Jews to be found in Susa, and hold a fast on my behalf, and neither eat nor drink for three days, night or day. I and my maids will also fast as you do. After that I will go to the king, though it is against the law; and if I perish, I perish.' Mordecai then went away and did everything as Esther had ordered him. (Esther 4:10-17, NRSV)

Esther summoned her courage and approached the king. Through a series of meetings and careful planning she not only wins the favor of the king but brings to light the advisor who plotted against her people. In the end, Mordecai and the Jewish people are saved. Esther had her plans. God had a purpose. Esther could never had known as she lived her quiet life with Mordecai that in just one year she would become queen and risk her life to save her people. As she and Mordecai made plans to approach the king, God's purposes were at work, having begun with Esther's placement in the castle. We see this in Mordecai's advice of "Perhaps you have come to royal dignity for just such a time as this." Perhaps, he says to Esther, you are where you are, in this moment, to be a part of God's purposes.

You make plans in your life. Sometimes they work out. Sometimes you are left wondering how you ended up so far away from what you intended. Our plans rise and fall. Our decisions and hopes are subject to both our own motivation and outside forces beyond our control. God's purposes, however, are unfailing. God ordains purposes for the world and its creation, for all of the people. God sees the scope of the whole world and sets a direction for its events. God, as in the life of Esther, also has a unique purpose for you.

What does this really mean? Some would argue that every plan, every decision, moments as small as what breakfast cereal you chose, are a part of God's plan in your life. Each event, from finding a parking spot to a major surgery, are individually ordained and created. Perhaps they are right.

What is of more concern for the discussion of Esther, however, are God's purposes. A discussion of God's purposes is less concerned with each individual decision or event in isolation, and more concerned with the overarching purpose of God in your life, and in the world. As we look at Esther, the day to day events were not recorded. Her plans for each individual moment were not of concern. What is of note are the times when she is placed for "just such a time as this." These were the events where Esther's plans intersected with God's purposes and her life was brought in line with the broader story of God's work in the world.

Some events or decisions in your life will be forgotten, unrecorded and insignificant. Entire weeks or even months may seem uneventful. But there will be other moments when you too are in the exact place God has brought you and have the opportunity to be a part of God's purpose. Your plans collide with God's work and the broader movement of the Spirit in the world is at work in your life. You throw your life at the mercy of God, and like Esther, have a chance to serve in ways you could hardly have imagined.

You have made plans in your life. Each day you make decisions, adjust to changes, and work toward these plans. But what is your purpose? God is at work in all sorts of ways and in all sorts of places. Plans are contingent on situations and choices. A plan can easily be thwarted by an unexpected change in schedule or an illness. As our plans come and go, what if God has uniquely equipped you to serve a purpose in your life, whether you are picking out cereal at the grocery store or heading to an appointment at rush hour? And how do we know what this purpose is?

Sometimes we can't. Esther could not have imagined at first that her placement as queen would be used in the salvation of God's people. She could not have anticipated the way things would unfold with the death of her parents, her relationship with Mordecai, her role as a Jew in the palace. Sometimes our participation in God's purposes will unfold as if outside of our control, and we chose to simply set our plans aside and participate as God's purposes become clear.

Other times we are able to mold and shape our plans to this very purpose of God in our life. Once Esther saw how God was at work, she participated in planning a series of steps to gain a hearing with the king. She acknowledges that her plans may fail, going so far as to say "if I perish, I perish." But knowing what God has purposed for her days, she reorients her life and her plans to this greater purpose.

Growing up we spent many weekends in the company of my great aunt, who we called Detah. Detah lived alone in a condo near the beach, but was rarely without company. It seemed like everywhere she went, people knew her. She was a hard woman to miss. I can still remember how the gold sequins that covered her flats would sparkle in the afternoon sunlight, sending reflections on to the walls around her. She always wore bright red lipstick that highlighted her huge smile. Our greeting was never short of a big kiss right on the lips. Her laugh was as bright as her shoes and she was always "stirring the pot" amongst her three siblings at family gatherings. We spent hours in her condo, watching the waves rise and fall in the Atlantic, playing cards and chatting about life. One particular visit, Detah mentioned that she needed some help cleaning around her home. Her spirit hadn't aged a bit but as her body grew older with each passing year, the tasks of scrubbing floors and dusting high shelves were proving more difficult. She began to make plans to hire someone to help. A few weeks later we returned and met her housekeeper. She was kind and soft spoken, and Detah adored her. There was just one small hiccup. The housekeeper was legally blind. At the time, this seemed to me to be a horrible plan. How would it be helpful to have someone clean her home that couldn't see? Why was she paying this woman to help her clean if she would end up doing much of the cleaning herself anyway? But to Detah it wasn't even a question. Her hiring of the woman had nothing to do with her plans and everything to do with her purpose. For years we had seen Detah reach out to the people around her, offering love and laughter and support. She was a woman of faith, and saw God in the faces of everyone around her. On her refrigerator hung a small drawing of a young girl, with the quote "I know I'm somebody, because God don't make no junk." Detah lived this way with everyone she met. No one was junk. Everyone was a child of God. This woman was no different. She had come across the woman and knew she needed a job. The housekeeper fit perfectly in line with her purpose of helping people. To Detah, it was obvious. The plans of house cleaning would be figured out another day.

We may see our plans as daily events, or at most working toward a yearly goal. What if we instead looked at how God might be at work in our life and adjusted our plans to this purpose? How do we start to see how God might use each of us? Take a look at your life. What passions do you have that might be gifts you could use to participate in God's work in the world? What are the needs around you that you just can't dismiss, and that you feel you could be a part of addressing? What have you been given that may be used to contribute to the good work being done? What have people in your life noticed about you? What place are you in right now, and why might that be?

As you look at these questions, you may see common threads emerge among your answers. In prayer and reflection, a purpose might emerge that can guide your plans and decisions. This is not to say God won't have other purposes in mind. But choosing to look for God's purpose in your life will make you open to the movement of God to direct your plans each step of the way. God has a purpose for the world. God has a purpose for you. Will you chose God's purpose over your plans?

Chapter 10
LOVE OVER HIDING
Toilet Charm Crush

In third grade, for the first time, I fell in love. And I fell hard. I can still remember watching him from across our classroom. He wore a striped t-shirt and had hair that hung just over his eyes while he worked. I had pigtails and a substantial overbite. That particular day I wore a blue and white stripped dress, white socks that folded over with a lace border, and red jellys, because jelly shoes were all the rage. Around my neck I wore a plastic charm necklace loaded with charms to trade with my friends. The most popular charms that week were the baby bottle and the toilet. I would peer over my work and watch the boy across the class. He wasn't the most handsome boy in our grade, or even the smartest, but my heart had chosen him. I would confide after school in my best friend Shannon, who would listen sympathetically behind her round pink glasses. I just knew we were supposed to get married and be together. Forever.

As time went on my love for him only grew, and I couldn't hold it back any longer. I sat at my desk for hours at home, writing, crossing out and crumpling up consecutive pieces of notebook paper until my trashcan was overflowing. Finally, after several attempts, I had a poem that was a derivative of "Roses are Red, Violets are Blue" that was signed from a secret admirer. I just knew that after a few of my love poems he would be so fascinated he would want to find out who wrote them and certainly go on a date. Maybe even get married.

The next morning in class offered the perfect opportunity to deliver my note. I was the first one to arrive and the classroom was empty. My jelly shoes clicking against the linoleum floors, I rushed over to his desk and slipped the note inside. I darted back to my desk and sat down, my cheeks burning, as the rest of the class filtered in. I could hardly focus the rest of the day. Who cared about times tables when he was sitting right across the room? Why hadn't he read the note? I watched carefully for the rest of the day but he gave no notice of the letter waiting for him.

The next day I thought I might need to up my game. I carefully penned another poem, and folded the note with a "pull here" tab. Just inside the folded flap of paper, I taped my prized toilet charm. I waited for another quiet moment in the classroom, tip toed to his desk and set it just inside, right in front of his stack of books, where I knew he couldn't miss it. Then I snuck back to my desk to wait for destiny. I didn't have to wait long. He walked in with his blond hair slightly mussed from the playground and fell in to his seat, his t-shirt sticky with sweat from a rowdy game of tag at recess. I waited, tapping my toes nervously, and trying not to stare. He reached his hand absent mindedly in to his desk to grab his trapper keeper and I saw with excitement that his hand emerged clutching a perfectly folded piece of notebook paper with a slight bulge in the side. It was my note! He opened it carelessly, slightly ripping the paper as it opened. His eyes scanned the poem then he crumpled it up and tossed it and the charm in the trash can. Along with my heart.

None of us are strangers to heartbreak. At first it was the crushing blow of rejection from our first love. Our heart yearned and we followed its leading only to find ourselves destroyed in the wake of being turned away by the object of our adoration. We went on to offer our hearts to both lovers and friends. We have spent sleepless nights imagining ourselves with that boy or girl whose voice makes our palms sweat and our heads feel fuzzy. We develop friendships with the love of those who have known our secrets and our hopes. Then one relationship at a time, we get our heart broken. There are the unique relationships were our heart stays protected, but for the rest we walk away hurt, our heart having been vulnerable once more to the whims of another. A romantic relationship ends. A friendship falls apart. Each time we find it is a little more difficult to love someone again. Is the heartbreak worth the love we experienced? Would it have been easier to chose to hide instead of love to begin with?

The women who were a part of Jesus' inner circle loved him. They didn't love him in a romantic way. They loved him as the son of God, their Messiah, their one true hope that things would be different. They had listened to his teachings and felt their hearts swell with excitement. The women had seen him heal and knew his claims were true. They had seen his care for the poor and the lost, the way he would teach and feed and heal the people until he collapsed in exhaustion at the end of the day. They loved him for how he lived and for who he was.

And now he was gone. In something out of their worst nightmares, he had been taken away from them. The man who had lived out love for others everyday he had walked among them had died as a criminal on the cross. They would never again hear his voice echoing over the crowds. They would never again witness the unspeakable joy of those he had healed. Their hearts were shattered. The despair was almost too much to endure. They shared stories they remembered about him. Their voices cracked and their eyes filled with tears. When there were no more words they sat in silence, wondering how they would go on. As they sat huddled together, there was soon an unspoken agreement of what they must do. It was time to go and prepare his body for burial. It felt impossible, to go to the tomb. They had loved him so much. It would have been so much easier to hide, to try to protect their hearts from more pain. But one at a time, they picked themselves up from the floor with a new determination. It is what he would have done. It is what love required. So they went.

> But on the first day of the week, at early dawn, they came to the tomb, taking the spices that they had prepared. They found the stone rolled away from the tomb, but when they went in, they did not find the body. While they were perplexed about this, suddenly two men in dazzling clothes stood beside them. The women were terrified and bowed their faces to the ground, but the men said to them, "Why do you look for the living among the dead? He is not here, but has risen. Remember how he told you, while he was still in Galilee, that the Son of Man must be handed over to sinners, and be crucified, and on the third day rise again." Then they remembered his words, and returning from the tomb, they told all this to the eleven and to all the rest. Now it was Mary Magdalene, Joanna, Mary the mother of James, and the other women with them who told this to the apostles. But these words seemed to them an idle tale, and they did not believe them. But Peter got up and ran to the tomb; stooping and looking in, he saw the linen cloths by themselves; then he went home, amazed at what had happened. (Luke 24:1-12, NRSV)

The women could have hidden. But instead they went to the tomb because their hearts continued to love in the midst of their despair. They had not given up on caring for Jesus, or for one another. Love meant pain, they knew that now, but it wouldn't stop them from continuing to reach out of themselves.

But something was wrong. The stone at the edge of the tomb had been moved. As they drew closer, they jumped as the glow of the angels appear beside them. The appearance of the angels was terrifying. Their minds were still fuzzy from shock and their hearts heavy from grief. What were the angels saying? The news felt too good to be true. He had risen. It had really happened. He really was the risen son of God. The words slowly sunk in through the outer shell of their pain and in to their consciousness. Their feet hit hard against the ground as they sprinted breathlessly to the disciples. The disciples didn't believe them at first. The women seemed confused by their pain and had a crazed excitement among them. But as Peter looked in to the tomb, he saw, as the women had seen, that Jesus' body was gone.

What would have happened if the women had let their heartbreak keep them from this offering of love for Jesus? What if they had chosen to hide together in their despair instead of coming to the tomb? They would have missed their opportunity to be the very first witnesses to the resurrection of the one they had loved and lost. The women chose love over hiding. At the tomb that day they found what God was doing and they felt the pieces of their lives start to come back together. Even though love meant vulnerability and pain, they chose to love again as they followed Christ.

You have had your heartbroken. Maybe you have even been tempted to hide from loving again. Love becomes a liability, it is just too painful. But God heals your broken heart. Psalm 147:3 says God "heals the brokenhearted and binds up their wounds." (NRSV) In a great act of love for us God collects the broken pieces of our lives when we have been hurt and puts them back together. These heartbreaks are much deeper than a rejected third grade crush. These are the deep hurts of a deceased spouse, a divorce, a destroyed long term friendship. Your heart aches as you try to figure out how you will start again, or even just get through the day today. These hurts leave scars as they heal. But God has called you to keep loving, one day at a time. God has called you out of hiding to offer your love for others as you are healed from your pain.

God can ask this of us because this is precisely what God has done for us. Whether intentionally or not, we attempt to break the heart of God. God offers to love us and we push God away. God shows us the way to live and we chose to go in the opposite direction. We reject God's laws and God's people. Yet, God decides to love us anyway, one day at a time, no matter how hard we might make it, no matter how unlovable we make ourselves out to be. God writes us a letter of love in the words of the Bible, and if we crumple it up, God sends it again and again in to our lives, through other people and other situations until we can't hide anymore from the love of God.

We are created in the image of this loving God. We are created to love, trying time and again to love others, no matter how much it costs us. Love doesn't always look the same way, and it certainly doesn't always mean charms and love poems. Sometimes love means drawing close and being vulnerable to those that we trust, even when it is hard. Sometimes love means ending a destructive relationship so that each person can find their own path to wholeness. Sometimes love means doing something risky to protect those entrusted to our care. Sometimes love means an openness to new relationships even when old ones still haunt our hearts. Hiding tempts us to stay in abusive situations, to live in the pain of the past, to shelter ourselves from openness with others. Love challenges us to be strong and open to where God leads. Love comes from courage. Hiding comes from fear. Love comes from the God whose love will never leave us.

We are called to come out of hiding and offer this kind of love to the world. Our love goes beyond just our personal relationships and reaches out to all people with the love God has shown us. We know the more we open up our lives, the more likely we are to be disappointed. We watch the news and we get discouraged. We try to help others in a new way and we fail. And so we hide. It is easier to hide in the security of our lives than to keep trying to reach out to the people around us. But this is precisely what God has done, and what we are called to do as disciples. Jesus did not hide behind the stone at the tomb. He rose again, in a great act of love for the people of the world, offering grace and hope for generations to come.

We may not be able to offer love for the entire world in one great act. But we can love people in the world around us, one at a time. There was a woman who had raised her daughter well. She provided healthy meals, good schools and a safe home. She knew she had taught her everything she could, and most importantly, had loved her with all of her heart. But children often break the hearts of their parents. Her daughter sat in their living room one night and told her mom that she was pregnant. She was just out of high school. She didn't have a job. She didn't have a husband. This was not the life her mom would have wanted for her. Her mom rehearsed everything they had done in her head. What could she have done differently to prevent this? What had happened? Hiding would have been so easy. She could have hidden from her daughter, pushing her aside and out of her life. She could have hidden from her friends and family who would undoubtedly have opinions about this turn of events. She could have hidden from this new reality that turned the life of her family upside down. But as she looked across the family room at her daughter that night, she made a choice. She chose to love. She loved her daughter as she went through the physical exhaustion of pregnancy. She loved her as she had to make decisions about her career and schooling. She threw her a baby shower. She bought her baby gifts. She held her granddaughter when her daughter was working to provide for her new young family. It was heartbreaking to see her daughter's life change so quickly. But she didn't hide. She loved her in the midst of it. By the grace of the God who loved her too.

Have you been holding back from loving the people around you fully because you have been heartbroken from a past hurt? Do you let a fear of being hurt keep you from caring for others in new relationships? Is there someone in your life that needs to experience God's love through you? How can you chose to live a life of love instead of hiding?

Chapter 11
PRESENT OVER PAST
Good on Paper

Get a job. These were the three words that ruled our lives the last few months of graduate school. We had taken all of the classes. We had done internships and taken ordination exams. Everything was in order. Except for one small final step. Get a job. For the first two and half years of graduate school we talked about ultimate frisbee and class schedules. We ate dinner at picnic tables while our kiddos crawled on blankets spread in the grass until the sun sank behind our small apartment buildings. Then we returned to our couches to study while watching reality television. Suddenly something shifted in those last few months. You could sense the tension in the air as we applied for positions, sometimes the same positions, and waited to hear back. In a matter of weeks we would be forced to leave the security of our seminary housing, and lose with it our home, health clinic, and community. We needed to Get. A. Job. Because the job in question was being a pastor, it definitely had a spiritual component. Conversations were full of phrases like "finding a call" and "discerning the next step." It is true that the search process for a pastoral position is a complicated, long process with a church where both parties are working to hear the voice of God as they look at paperwork, have phone conversations, and eventually meet one another. But there are also the practical concerns of health insurance and salary negotiations that fall in the job column of the conversation.

My husband and I interviewed for various pastoral positions. As graduation loomed near we had two churches that were serious, one in New York City and one in Iowa. We went back and forth between the two, praying for direction, weighing the pros and cons, and visited each. In the end, we packed up our belongings and drove west to Iowa.

Our experience there can be best compared to a failed relationship where both parties have the best intentions. They were a good church. It was a large congregation with energetic volunteers and a substantial staff and budget. We were well intentioned pastors. We had the naiveté and idealism of two recent graduates, but we were excited and ready to serve. We bought a house and moved to town with our tiny u-haul, our two newly minted degrees and our one year old son.

Sometimes in a relationship with two well intentioned parties things just don't work out. We were, unfortunately, in one of those relationships. Within weeks of starting in ministry there we sensed it was not a good fit for us, or for the church. We also discovered that we were pregnant with our second child. With a mortgage and one and half children to feed, we started the application process, to get a job, again.

The next few months were tough. We announced to the church we were leaving. We felt terrible, they felt terrible, no one was surprised. We spent late nights sitting in our living room fretting over how we would provide for our children. We were thousands of miles from our friends and our family and were about to have a new baby. We felt the failure of leaving our first jobs so soon. We had never felt quite so alone. By the end of the year we sold our house and lost our down payment. We loaded up our belongings again, this time with two children in tow, and moved to Ohio to start over. We left with pain in our hearts and a general feeling of regret that dogged us for months. It had seemed like we had done everything right. We had worked hard in school, completed our requirements, found a church placement. Then in our very first attempt at finding the right match we had ended up lost. Now we had to start over with less money and a shred of our confidence left intact.

The years passed and we both found our rhythm as pastors with churches that were a fit for each of us. Iowa became a distant memory. We let go of the feelings of hurt and confusion that had clouded that year and tried to forget. But with us we cherished a small reminder of our short lived home in Iowa who grew older with each passing birthday, who we saw as the blessing of what had been a difficult year. As he grew older, he began to ask to visit his birthplace. We had, after all, made trips back to New Jersey where his brother was born. Finally we realized it was time, and we headed west.

We drove in to town and passed through familiar streets and neighborhoods. We visited the house where we brought him home as a baby. We went to our favorite ice cream shop. We drove down our old street. We were unprepared for the emotion that would catch in our throats as we toured the town we had not returned to since we left with all of our belongings to move to our new home. My husband and I didn't say much, but I see the memories flooding over him as they were over me. We held back the emotion with what we hoped were convincing smiles.

That evening we had dinner with a couple we had not seen since we moved. They graciously invited us to stay in their home. The first few minutes were painfully awkward. We weren't sure what to say to the people who had been our closest friends there, but who we had not seen in eight years. It didn't take long for our younger son, our Iowa native, to break through the tension with a moment of awful, beautiful honesty. "My parents said I am the only good thing to come out of Iowa."

Oh Lord. My husband and I sat mute. In one clear, unnuanced statement, our son had summarized our struggle with the past. He had unintentionally parroted our pain. We hadn't realized he had picked up on our perspective of his home town. We were stunned and unsure how to recover the conversation. But to our relief, our hosts laughed, and we followed suit. The next few hours offered a healing we did not realize we needed. We talked about their lives and the current ministries at the church where we had served there. We shared about our kids and heard about theirs. They asked about our lives in Ohio. We played cards until late in to the evening hours.

The next day we drove back down those same roads, but they were different now. The familiar houses and storefronts had brought back painful memories the day before. They had been reminders of a past that had followed us. Now they were simply a piece of our story. This was just a town, a place that had once held a difficult situation, but was also a place to celebrate the birth of our youngest son. We had found healing. We had started to let go of the past. And now we were able to start a new life in the present.

Our past shapes who we are, especially the harder times. We look back at failed jobs, failed relationships, unexpected grief and hardship and we know these are the very things that have made us who we are. We share true but overused cliches like "what doesn't kill us makes us stronger." But if we are honest, the hardship of our past doesn't necessarily leave us unscathed. The strength we gained through the low points of the years past has come with a cost.

Hagar was on the run from her past. She was the slave of Sarai and Abram, who we later know as Sarah and Abraham. Sarah and Abraham were promised children by the Lord. Hagar had overheard them talking about it. They had been promised to parent the generations of God's people. She had seen Sarah change from elation to desperation as the time went by and there was no child. Sarah was still not pregnant.

> Now Sarai, Abram's wife, bore him no children. She had an Egyptian slave-girl whose name was Hagar, and Sarai said to Abram, 'You see that the Lord has prevented me from bearing children; go in to my slave-girl; it

may be that I shall obtain children by her.' And Abram listened to the voice of Sarai. So, after Abram had lived for ten years in the land of Canaan, Sarai, Abram's wife, took Hagar the Egyptian, her slave-girl, and gave her to her husband Abram as a wife. He went in to Hagar, and she conceived; and when she saw that she had conceived, she looked with contempt on her mistress. (Genesis 16:1-4, NRSV)

Hagar might have known she shouldn't have looked at Sarah that way. But Sarah has used her to get the child she was promised. She had pulled Hagar in to her attempts to further the promise from the Lord in her impatience. She knew she had been too proud when Sarah had walked by. She should not have taunted her mistress with her swelling belly. But it was too late.

Then Sarai said to Abram, 'May the wrong done to me be on you! I gave my slave-girl to your embrace, and when she saw that she had conceived, she looked on me with contempt. May the Lord judge between you and me!' But Abram said to Sarai, 'Your slave-girl is in your power; do to her as you please.' Then Sarai dealt harshly with her, and she ran away from her. (Genesis 16:5-6, NRSV)

Now Hagar was on the run from her past. She had crossed her already crazed mistress, and now Abraham had abandoned her to Sarai's will. She couldn't live anymore with the woman who looked at her with such contempt. She couldn't bear the anger and the pain. Hagar ran deep in to the wilderness. The branches swept by her face and her legs ached but she kept running. She ran from the hatred of Sarai. She ran from the betrayal of Abram. She ran from the fear of what would happen to her and her child now. Then finally she could not run anymore, and she dropped to her feet in exhaustion by a spring of water.

The angel of the Lord found her by a spring of water in the wilderness, the spring on the way to Shur. And he said, 'Hagar, slave-girl of Sarai, where have you come from and where are you going?' She said, 'I am running away from my mistress Sarai.' The angel of the Lord said to her, 'Return to your mistress, and submit to her.' The angel of the Lord also said to her, 'I will so greatly multiply your offspring that they cannot be counted for multitude.' And the angel of the Lord said to her,
'Now you have conceived and shall bear a son;
  you shall call him Ishmael,
  for the Lord has given heed to your affliction.

He shall be a wild ass of a man,
with his hand against everyone,
   and everyone's hand against him;
and he shall live at odds with all his kin.'
So she named the Lord who spoke to her, 'You are El-roi'; for she said,
'Have I really seen God and remained alive after seeing him?' Therefore
the well was called Beer-lahai-roi; it lies between Kadesh and Bered. Hagar
bore Abram a son; and Abram named his son, whom Hagar bore, Ishmael.
Abram was eighty-six years old when Hagar bore him Ishmael. (Genesis
16:7-16, NRSV)

Hagar could run from Sarai and Abram. She could even run from her past. But
she couldn't run from the Lord. In an amazing moment in her story, she is met
face to face by her God. She must have been stunned. No one ever saw the
Lord. Or at least they didn't live to tell about it. Here she was, a pregnant slave
girl, on the run from her mistress, hidden deep in the wilderness. She was
convinced no one knew where she was, and that no one cared if they did. She
was alone and scared and ready to die. She had a past that she couldn't control
and a future that seemed impossible. Then the Lord appears to her. The Lord
tells her to return to Sarai and Abram, and that the Lord will multiply her
offspring. After the Lord leaves, she offers the name "El-roi" and returns back
home.

Hagar could not change her past. Her life had been hard, and she may have
been tempted to just stay in the wilderness. When she returned she knew she
would have to face what had happened to her. She would have to let go of what
she had experienced. But the Lord had promised her a new present. The Lord
had promised that she was not alone, and that the future had possibilities for
her and her child. Hagar took the first step toward healing. Taking a deep
breath, she picked herself up off the ground, wiping the mud from her knees.
She summoned her courage and headed back toward her home, prepared to let
go of the past and live in the present offered to her.

You have a past that has shaped you. Perhaps there are things you aren't proud
of. Maybe there are events or relationships you would do anything to change.
You can't. You can't change what has happened, no matter how many times it is
replayed or rehashed. You can't change the events that have unfolded or the
choices that were made. You can't run from the things you have experienced no
matter how far you go. Because the God of your past is the God of your
present. The same God who you have known in the years that have come and

gone is the one who meets you in the wilderness. This God will not rewind time and change what has happened. God can, however, offer you a chance to live today. God offers you a chance to let go of your past and fully live in your present, open to what that might be.

This is not easy. We know the past is unchangeable, and yet we convince ourselves that if we just think through it one more time it might make sense. We hold onto past hurts thinking if we let them go then it makes what happened okay. Sometimes we can let go of the past on our own, seeking God's strength to move on from what we have experienced. Sometimes our past haunts have such a hold that we need to partner with a therapist who can walk with us through our healing. Letting go takes courage as we face the harder times of our lives. We can find the courage to do this with God's help. This may be working on our hearts to release the pain of the past. It may be leaving an unhealthy relationship that has dictated our past but cannot determine our future. It could be reaching out with a word of apology to a family member where there has been pain. Letting go can mean retelling our story to integrate the past as a part of what we have lived through but not what defines who we are today.

It also takes persistence. When Hagar returned home, she would have to face reminders of her past everyday. Living in the present was not a one time choice to leave the wilderness, but a daily decision to not run again. For many of us, it will take persistence over a period of days or even years to move on. Reminders of a person or a situation will pop up, sometimes when we least expect it, and throw us back in to our memories. A photograph buried in a stack of papers, the date on the calendar or even the smell of a familiar recipe will hijack our minds back to a time years ago. With God's help, we once again let go of our past and refocus on the day in front of us. Perhaps as we find healing we begin to see how the past has brought us where we are and shaped who we have become.

What are the things in your past that you have held on to? What are the past hurts that make you want to run? Are these memories keeping you from living fully today? What are steps you could take to find healing with God's help?

Chapter 12
RECONCILIATION OVER PRIDE
Pizza Man Betrayal

I skipped school. It was seventh grade and it was the first time it had occurred to me that leaving school was even an option. Until that point I had assumed the only option was to go to school, stay there, then return home on the bus. I had a couple of friends who blew apart my world view by suggesting that we could, in fact, leave mid morning. I should have said "No. Skipping school is wrong. I want to learn." I actually said "Okay! Meet you outside after first period!"

Not one to do something halfway, we decided that not only would we skip class, but we would walk the two miles back to my house, knowing my parents would not be home. In this one decision, I had chosen to break three different absolute rules in my house. Skipping school was definitely forbidden. That was a given. I was also not allowed to walk home. It was a busy street without sidewalks and went through an area of town with a known drug problem. Another long standing rule in our house was that we could not have a friend over of the opposite gender without adults present. One of the friends happened to be a boy. In a household with only five or six important rules, breaking three of them in one outing was quite a feat.

We walked the busy road toward my neighborhood, balancing precariously on the edge of the rain ditch on the side of the road. Our paranoia increased as we walked. Every police officer was looking for us. Every red sedan was my parent's Toyota. I began to wonder if this had been a huge mistake. Thirty minutes later, we arrived on my front doorstep, sweaty and exhausted but unscathed.

I let my friends in to the house. For a few moments we were overtaken with the nervous giddiness of doing something sneaky. We flopped down on the cool carpet floor to rest. When the butterflies in our stomachs subsided, we realized we were starving. With the lack of forethought that comes with early adolescence, we had not planned on what we would do for lunch. Our first idea was to set off again, on foot, to the fast food taco restaurant closest to my home. This was a time before cell phones and GPS, and we ended up traveling in circles on the dirt roads of my neighborhood. We remained determined until we ran into a large fence blocking our path with a sign warning of a dangerous dog living on the other side of the barrier.

Disheartened, we headed back to my house to regroup. In a stroke of genius, one of my friends cried "Let's order a pizza!" Ordering pizza on a normal Friday night was enough to excite us. Ordering a warm, cheesy pizza while skipping school was the stuff of legend. We watched eagerly out the front window for the delivery car to arrive. The adult delivering the pizza looked at us skeptically as we counted out waded up one dollar bills and pressed it into his hand. We grabbed the pizza and quickly shut and locked the door behind us.

We laughed over the steaming slices, picturing our friends trapped back in the school cafeteria picking at their mystery meat school lunch. As we lay there on the floor, our bellies full and our faces gleaming with grease, we had another moment of clarity. We needed to be back in time to catch the bus home or our parents would be notified we weren't on the bus. We scrambled to our feet, shoving on our shoes and rearranging the couch cushions to appear untouched. The pizza box was carefully discarded in a trash can several houses down. We left no trace of our crime, and made the walk back to school in record time.

It was unbelievable. We had gotten away with it. I rode the bus home chatting excitedly with friends and sharing stories of our adventure during the day. Deep down, my unease had started to grow. I knew I would have to lie to my parents. I assured myself that I wouldn't have to tell a lie, per say. I would merely need to neglect to share the details of my day. I walked nervously through my front door, and was greeted promptly by my mother. She called distractedly from the kitchen "Hi sweetie! How was your day?" "Good!" I called back, a little too eagerly, and sprinted back to my room under the guise of homework.

The hours passed and life felt normal. I felt a rush of pride as I realized what we had accomplished that day. I summoned my courage and headed in to the kitchen, where my mom was making dinner. As soon as I sat down on the barstool at our counter, the phone rang. I dashed to grab it in case it was a friend.
"Hello?"
"Yes, is this the customer who ordered a pizza from us today?"
I froze. My heart pounded and I started to sweat. My mom looked up at me quizzically and I made a gesture that I hoped communicated it was just a telemarketer. I leaned over the phone, cupping my hand over the mouthpiece to quiet my voice.

"Yes it is." I whispered.

"We were just calling to see how you liked your pizza?"

"Um, it was fine. Thanks. Goodbye." I threw the phone back into its receiver and slowly turned around.

"Who was that?" my mom asked slowly.

"Um. No one. Nothing."

"Because earlier someone called and asked how we liked our pizza that we ordered? I told them we hadn't ordered a pizza, but they assured me we had?"

She knew. We had been betrayed by the pizza delivery man. Maybe we should have given him a better tip. The story tumbled out of me in a matter of minutes. How we had decided to skip school. How we walked home. How I had broken house rules one after the other. I was grounded. For the entirety of Spring Break. I don't remember much about that week (there wasn't much to remember since I couldn't leave the house). But I do remember the reaction of my parents. After their initial "we are disappointed in you talk", there seemed to be a lightening of their mood. It wasn't that I was off the hook. Far from it. Grounding was serious business in my house, which meant no phones, no music, no friends, no television. Watching paint dry would have been a nice change of pace. But as my boredom grew, so did my wounded pride. I had thought we were clever enough to get away with it, but we had failed. I distanced myself from my parents, nursing my wounded ego that they had discovered my treachery. One afternoon I came skulking in to the kitchen and noticed a note for me on the counter. It was a post it, asking if I needed a snack. The post it was attached to a pizza coupon, for the very company that had betrayed my friends and I. Well played, mom and dad. I laughed quietly in spite of myself. As I laughed, I felt my pride give way. Despite the fact that I had broken every house rule, despite my pouting, they still wanted a relationship with me.

Living in relationship with other people isn't always easy. A husband and wife don't always see eye to eye. Parents and children are at odds over rules or plans. Coworkers compete for the same promotion. Friendships become strained by different directions in life. We see the tension build in these relationships. We struggle to know how we will overcome the latest disagreement and live together again. Our pride tells us it is more important to be right than to find common ground. We replay the situations over and over again in our minds, convincing ourselves of our innocence. But we know we have to find a way to reconcile. These are the people that are most important to us. They are what give our life purpose and meaning.

Sometimes we even find our pride gets in the way of our relationship with God. Something happens that we don't understand. We have been praying for answers but we just can't seem to see how God is at work. We know we have chosen the wrong path in our lives but can't admit it to ourselves, let alone seek God's forgiveness. Our pride increases the distance we feel from God and days turn in to weeks since we have spent any time reflecting on our faith.

Miriam had every reason to feel proud. She had seen a lot with her brothers in following God. When Moses was just a baby, she had placed him in a river, floating in a basket, and watched to make sure he was safe. She heard years later about his call from God to free the people of Israel, and how the Lord spoke to him in a burning bush. She was there when the waters of the Red Sea formed two fantastic columns, leaving a narrow pathway between them for her people to pass to safety. She watched in awe as the water came crashing down behind them to drown their pursuers. She was knows as a prophetess, and her song is recorded in the Bible alongside the stories of Moses. She continued with her brothers and the people as they wandered in the wilderness. Recently the people were grumbling and becoming discontent. The memory of their dramatic salvation from slavery had faded with each passing day. They were exhausted. They were hungry. They were starting to doubt that they would ever arrive in the promised land. They had even begun to think that things were better when they were in slavery.

The people weren't the only ones beginning to show the strain of their exhaustion. Miriam and Aaron may have wondered why no one listened to them. Miriam was a prophetess, after all. Had they not been there every step of the way? Didn't they deserve some credit as leaders too? The pair's pride increased and they began to whisper together. It wasn't long before their relationship with their brother became tense with the rivalry of siblings. The grumbling of the people finally took its tole on Miriam who spoke out in a moment of frustration against Moses.

> "While they were at Hazeroth, Miriam and Aaron spoke against Moses because of the Cushite woman whom he had married (for he had indeed married a Cushite woman); and they said, 'Has the Lord spoken only through Moses? Has he not spoken through us also?' "(Numbers 12:1-2, NRSV)

As soon as the words came out of her mouth Miriam regretted what she had done. She clapped her hand over her mouth. But it was too late. The damage had been done.

"And the Lord heard it. Now the man Moses was very humble, more so than anyone else on the face of the earth. Suddenly the Lord said to Moses, Aaron, and Miriam, 'Come out, you three, to the tent of meeting.' So the three of them came out. Then the Lord came down in a pillar of cloud, and stood at the entrance of the tent, and called Aaron and Miriam; and they both came forward. And he said, 'Hear my words: When there are prophets among you,

   I the Lord make myself known to them in visions;
   I speak to them in dreams.
Not so with my servant Moses;
   he is entrusted with all my house.
With him I speak face to face—clearly, not in riddles;
   and he beholds the form of the Lord.
Why then were you not afraid to speak against my servant Moses?' And the anger of the Lord was kindled against them, and he departed." When the cloud went away from over the tent, Miriam had become leprous, as white as snow. And Aaron turned towards Miriam and saw that she was leprous. Then Aaron said to Moses, 'Oh, my lord, do not punish us for a sin that we have so foolishly committed. Do not let her be like one stillborn, whose flesh is half consumed when it comes out of its mother's womb.' And Moses cried to the Lord, 'O God, please heal her.' But the Lord said to Moses, 'If her father had but spat in her face, would she not bear her shame for seven days? Let her be shut out of the camp for seven days, and after that she may be brought in again.' So Miriam was shut out of the camp for seven days; and the people did not set out on the march until Miriam had been brought in again. After that the people set out from Hazeroth, and camped in the wilderness of Paran." (Numbers 12:2-16, NRSV)

Miriam wasn't totally off base. She had followed the Lord in to risky places, just like Moses. She had been there when the seas were parted, just like Moses. She had heard the word of God, maybe not face to face, but just as Moses had. But in a moment of weakness she let her pride get the best of her. Her sense of accomplishment became a weapon to use against her brother, and she suffered for her actions.

Her return to camp cannot have been easy. The people had watched for her for seven days as she waited for her skin to return to normal. What had been a comment meant only for Aaron's ears had become an object of public shame. There was no way to hide what she had done. Her pride could have kept her from returning to the camp. She could have told herself that Moses deserved her scorn and that she was suffering unfairly. Moses, the perfect brother, who saved the people from slavery. Moses, the famous one, who had talked to the Lord in a burning bush. But he really had married that Cushite woman, and he shouldn't have. Maybe she shouldn't have gossiped about it. That part she wasn't proud of. And now the whole camp knew what had happened. She could have decided to go off on her own rather than face a return to the people. But the text tells us Miriam came back. Miriam chose to set aside her wounded pride and reconcile with her brother. She chose Moses and Aaron. She chose the people. She chose the relationships. Miriam chose reconciliation over pride.

Miriam had very good reasons to be frustrated. Many of us in her position would have found ourselves just as she had, exiled temporarily from the camp for gossiping against our brother. We may find ourselves today in a position where our relationship has fallen apart, like Miriam's. Sometimes it is a small disagreement. Then what started as an insignificant argument spirals in to a situation that threatens to break apart what is left of the relationship. Sometimes it is one event that flips everything upside down. We rage. We dwell. We make a list of all that we have done right and the other party has done wrong. Our pride rises to our defense, encouraging us to sacrifice our connection with others before the altar of being right.

As we storm around outside the camp, God calls us to let go and start again. God undoubtedly worked in Miriam's heart in those seven days. Maybe she was right to be frustrated about her brother. But what was she willing to give up? Was she willing to lose the closeness with her brothers and the love of her people? Was protecting her pride worth losing everyone she loved? God works in our hearts too. Are we willing to sacrifice someone in our lives because our pride says we are right? What will we lose if we insist on maintaining the walls between ourselves and others instead of doing the work of reconciliation?

Reconciliation comes in lots of different ways. For Miriam it meant walking back to the camp at the end of her long week of exile ready to start fresh with Moses and her people. Reconciliation can be like Miriam's, a physical return to those we have been separated from. We may have to make a physical trip back home to rebuild a relationship we have lost. It can also be an apology. It can be a phone call as the first one to reach out and attempt to start over together. It can be moving one hand slowly toward the other during an argument until your fingers meet.

Sometimes reconciliation together is impossible. A relationship has become abusive or dangerous, and one party must walk away. This is not pride. This is running from evil in to the safety of God's care. Reconciliation does not mean being a doormat, and releasing pride does not mean we don't take steps to protect ourselves or those we love who are created in God's image. In cases like these, reconciliation comes from letting go of past pain and moving forward, separately. In these cases, instead of returning to camp we set out in a new direction, the work of reconciliation happening as God heals our hearts from past hurt as we start fresh.

Other times reconciliation only seems impossible. One day my husband, who is also a pastor, came home from a coffee shop in our town and shared about a man he had just met. His name was Laurent, and he and Dave had struck up a conversation while waiting for their coffee, and ended up getting to know a bit about one another. Laurent shared that he was from a town in Rwanda and was in the United States raising funding and awareness for their redevelopment after the genocide in the 1990s. Over the course of the next few years, we learned more about the country of Rwanda and its past from Laurent as Dave worked with him.

There are many stories that could be shared about Laurent and the community in Rwanda for which he was building support. It has been amazing to see their work developing education, healthcare and self sufficiency for the villages. One of the most profound set of stories have been not the depictions of the genocide, which are equally powerful and horrific. The story of the genocide is now not an unfamiliar one, and was documented and shared here in the states by many over the past twenty years. What was a new perspective was to hear about the current work of reconciliation there in people's relationships. During the genocide, one tribe turned on another, instigating an explosion of violence. The tribe that led the attacks turned neighbor against neighbor, friend against friend. Communities that had lived peacefully together were now torn apart by bloodshed and devastation. But years after the genocide had ended, something astounding started happening. One person at a time, there was reconciliation. Family members of those killed in the genocide consented to meet with those who had murdered their loved ones. Communities sprung up with homes next door to each other containing members of the two different tribes. It is difficult, painful, slow work. There is still much more to be done. Certainly the atrocities of the past cannot be swept aside with platitudes. But in the middle of the devastation, despite the heartache and destruction of families and communities, the people of Rwanda chose what seemed impossible. Over time, friends who had been made enemies met back together. One day at a time, the community began to rebuild. One relationship at a time, they began to heal. Instead of pride, they chose, through the power of God's grace, to start the hard, long work of reconciliation. They chose to come back to the camp and try again.

Reconciliation is just that, work. It takes conscious effort and is often not accomplished all at once. It is also dependent on the strength of God. We are told to hold our ground, to prove our point. Rebuilding relationships is counter cultural, and may even be presented as the weaker choice, although it is in reality the much more difficult. The more difficult the controversy, the more of a battle it takes to rebuild. It is the kind of work that is only possible as we seek God's grace and openness through prayer and the support of others.

Reconciliation doesn't happen all at once, but never happens without a first step. Is there someone in your life that you could take one step toward in reconciliation? What in your pride would have to be set aside in order to try? Is there a relationship that has been strained by past events that you could work to rebuild if you could chose reconciliation over pride?

Chapter 13
LAUGHTER OVER UNDERSTANDING
Youth Camp Shennanigans

Working with teenagers has its own unique set of rewards. They are motivated and compassionate, despite what the media might tell you. I have stood alongside of students in sixth grade through high school as they served food to the homeless and built houses for those in poverty. They are also some of the most accepting people I know. At least for the particular group of young adults with whom I have the privilege of working with, connections are made regardless of sexuality or mental health or family background. Teenagers also have an impressive amount of energy and can seem to subsist on only soda and Doritos for days. Some of my most intense time with the adolescent set has been when we have traveled to youth camps in the summer, and I always come home revived and impressed by these young people.

For all of their maturity, teens are also trapped in the in-between world of no longer children and not quite adult. I believe this leaves them with a twinkle of mischief in their eyes that is entertaining but also leads them in to trouble. We were on day five of a six day trip at camp. The usually peaceful mountain campus was streaming with enthusiastic high school students. Frisbees flew through grass fields, paddle boats circled the lake's shores. Groups of teens crossed between buildings wearing matching t-shirts, arms linked together. In the evenings they gathered in one giant hall and sang Christian songs with beautiful, pure harmonies. On the last night, the songs lingered longer and tradition pulled us down around the lake. The darkness gave way to the passing of candlelight through the hundreds of students until the flames danced in the moonlight, glimmering on the lake's still surface. As I looked at the students around me, the candlelight highlighting their faces, I felt a surge of gratitude. While other adult leaders looked haggard after a week of intervening between arguing students I stood proudly with a group that had been nothing but a pleasure to travel with.

The candles blew out and the students embraced one another with hugs and tears, then we made our way back to the dorms to rest for the return drive home the next morning. As I prepared to head upstairs, I paused, noticing two things. The first was the glimmer of mischief now dancing in the eyes of one of the senior boys, replacing the candle's flame from moments before. The second was a water balloon peeking out of his pocket.

Exhaustion called me to retreat to my room, and as I said goodnight to the students, I casually mentioned that perhaps a good spot to watch for other returning students might be just outside the main doors. Looking back, I should not have encouraged them, but sleep deprivation had my guard down. With a wink, I was off to bed. I laid on the firm mattress and listened to the shrieks and singing of the teens in the night slowly give way to the quiet of curfew. I drifted in and out of a fitful sleep, trying to rest for the drive but finding the dinner time coffee I had consumed refusing to let my mind slip in to dreams. A few hours later, my phone made a low buzz. On its bright screen, a notification appeared. I had been tagged in a photo.

Perhaps it was a photo of the candle service that night, or the frisbee game from earlier that afternoon. I opened the notification and saw an unfamiliar scene on the screen. It was a picture of eight of the members of the youth group traveling with me. Their surroundings were as dark as the window in my room, lit only by the police car behind them. I sat upright. Police car? My eyes scanned frantically to the bottom of the photo. It was posted just ten minutes ago.

My mind was racing. I didn't understand. Weren't these the same kids who I had been so proud of just hours earlier? Why would they had left the camp? Didn't they know how much trouble they could be in? What would I tell their parents? Would I have to bail them out of jail? Would we be allowed to come back to the camp? Had anyone been hurt? How had water balloons turned in to an arrest? I just didn't understand.

I jumped up from my bed, threw on my clothes and grabbed my phone. I sent a text to the students, who were supposed to be sleeping in the rooms on my hall, requesting their presence. As I moved out of my room into the bright florescent light of the hallway, I heard eight sets of feet scrambling frantically upstairs from the dorm lobby. They fell breathlessly out of the stairwell, trying to look casual. Their eyes met mine, and I said quietly "Tell me a story about a police car." They looked panicked at one another and made a subtle movement backward leaving the oldest boy, a senior, at the head of the pack to explain.

"Well you see" he said "it all started with the water balloons." They unfolded a tale that became the subject of youth group legend. In their defense, they had followed my suggestion, and stood at the front entrance with their water balloons, waiting for unsuspecting other youth groups to return. When curfew fell, the call of the night lured them away from the dorm and out in to the camp ground. Their tale included adventures of running from a bat that was swooping through the dorm, waving a flag in the darkness of a field, and eating some abandoned pizza. They had wandered the camp grounds, the wet grass coating their athletic shoes and the silence of the night broken only by their giggling. As they approached a road in the camp, their hearts stopped. A police car approached. The police were used to the presence of the teens during the summer months, and they were also well informed about the hour of curfew. They were busted.

The officer exited his car and walked toward the eight students, who were now rooted in place like statues. The police officer spoke, his southern accent and kind face putting them more at ease. "Aren't you all out past curfew?" "Yes sir," they murmured. "Maybe you should head back to your rooms now then." The group scrambled to get ready to leave when the boy with the water balloon spoke. "Sir? Would it be okay if we took a picture with your squad car?"

There was a lot I didn't understand. Why had they broken one of the very few rules I held for them in leaving the dorm building? Why had they risked their own safety in being out alone at night? Why had they had the audacity to ask a police officer if they could take a picture with the squad car? And why, above all, had they then tagged me in the picture?

I sent them off to bed with a look of reproach and a stern lecture. They had never seen me this serious before, and it had its desired effect. They retreated to their rooms, heads hung low, and the hallway was silent. My mind replayed the story from start to finish. So much of it didn't make sense. So much of it baffled my adult sense of sensibility. So much of it was . . . . hysterical. I returned to my room with images of water balloons and bats and pizza. I tried to stifle my laughter so they wouldn't hear me, and drifted in to a restful sleep.

There was a lot Sarah did not understand. Sarah knew that the Lord had spoken to Abraham. She knew that they were supposed to become the parents of the generations to come. Abraham had come back from his encounter with God just bursting to tell her. They had made plans, dreamed of what the future would be like. But days turned in to months, and months turned in to years, and there were no children she could call her own. The subject had become tense to talk about between she and Abraham, and it became the unspoken wall that divided the two of them as the time passed. In the beginning, Sarah had prayed with joy and anticipation to the Lord about the next phase in her life. But now, her prayers were strained. Her confusion left her silent. Why would God have promised this to her and not brought it to pass? She was now too old for it to even be a possibility for them. What would happen next?

Late one afternoon, Abraham came running in to their tent. He spoke excitedly about the three men that would join them for rest and refreshment. Something in his tone said that these were not just any three men. They were in fact representative of the Lord. The same Lord who had promised their future. The same Lord who had seemingly abandoned them. He asked her to begin making the cakes as he dashed out of the door to get the milk. It wasn't long before he joined the men outside to sit and talk with them. Sarah peered curiously from the tent, straining to hear their conversation.

As Sarah listened, the talk turned to the promised children. Her heart flipped. As the years passed she had given up on God, sure that she was forgotten. Maybe they had misunderstood, maybe it was just not meant to be. But now the promise had resurfaced.

The Lord appeared to Abraham by the oaks of Mamre, as he sat at the entrance of his tent in the heat of the day. He looked up and saw three men standing near him. When he saw them, he ran from the tent entrance to meet them, and bowed down to the ground. He said, 'My lord, if I find favor with you, do not pass by your servant. Let a little water be brought, and wash your feet, and rest yourselves under the tree. Let me bring a little bread, that you may refresh yourselves, and after that you may pass on— since you have come to your servant.' So they said, 'Do as you have said.' And Abraham hastened into the tent to Sarah, and said, 'Make ready quickly three measures of choice flour, knead it, and make cakes.' Abraham ran to the herd, and took a calf, tender and good, and gave it to the servant, who hastened to prepare it. Then he took curds and milk and the calf that he had prepared, and set it before them; and he stood by them under the tree while they ate.

They said to him, 'Where is your wife Sarah?' And he said, 'There, in the tent.' Then one said, 'I will surely return to you in due season, and your wife Sarah shall have a son.' And Sarah was listening at the tent entrance behind him. Now Abraham and Sarah were old, advanced in age; it had ceased to be with Sarah after the manner of women. So Sarah laughed to herself, saying, 'After I have grown old, and my husband is old, shall I have pleasure?' The Lord said to Abraham, 'Why did Sarah laugh, and say, "Shall I indeed bear a child, now that I am old?" Is anything too wonderful for the Lord? At the set time I will return to you, in due season, and Sarah shall have a son.' But Sarah denied, saying, 'I did not laugh'; for she was afraid. He said, 'Oh yes, you did laugh.' (Genesis 18:1-15, NRSV)

Before looking at Sarah's reaction, a side note must be made regarding her situation in light of our modern perspective. Unlike early readers of the Biblical text, we have a full understanding of the challenges posed by infertility. We know the science behind the procreation of children, and we are well versed on fertility treatments and options. Most of us have seen the personal side of these struggles as well. Either you or someone you know has likely faced the deep pain that can come with infertility or miscarriage. The pain of this struggle for both women and men is real and cannot be casually brushed aside. Our temptation becomes to either ignore Biblical texts such as this story about Sarah, or to hold them up as proof of miracles. We know that infertility for some is a temporary obstacle to be overcome, but that for others will not be resolved by either scientific intervention or a miracle like Sarah's. It would be naive of us to read this story and think that every story has the happy ending of a child being born.

God loves each woman individually, just as she is, and the ability to carry children is no more an indication of the unique blessing of God than having freckles. In the same way, infertility is not a sign of God's punishment. Life happens, everyday and to each of us, as flesh and blood human beings on this giant rock flying through space. We are loved and cared for by God. And miracles do still happen. But how and why they occur is not something any of us can presume to predict, and is certainly not mathematically on scale with our holiness or number of people on the prayer chain. We pray because in some great mystery we cannot possibly comprehend God hears our cries and is at work in our life. We pray and feel God with us, working in our midst and through our struggles, including those in having children. There is no easy answer to the "why." An apparently perfectly suited couple remain childless and another couple becomes pregnant with a child they never wanted. Why? A pregnancy suddenly ends and the child doesn't survive. Why? We don't know. What we do know is that God is with us, in our joys and in our pain, and brings to us people to offer support as we move ahead. Bible stories like Sarah's challenge us with miracles we may never see. But Sarah's story, complicated though it may be, still offers a word for us today.

As we return to Sarah we look at her story not because of her fertility success. We look because she is lifted up as a woman who has an encounter with God, whose story is recorded in the Scriptures for the ages to come. For our purposes here, we look at Sarah not because of what is in her womb but what comes out of her mouth. It had been years since the prophecy that she will be the mother of the promised generations to come. The years had aged her body and broken her heart. She just didn't understand how it could possibly be true that she would carry a child. She didn't understand why the Lord would come now, after all of this time, and tell her she would become pregnant. How could this be true? She could have asked hundreds of questions. Sarah had a lot of years worth of doubt and confusion to clear up, and this was her chance. But instead of seeking to understand, Sarah simply takes it all in. Then she laughs. The motive of her laughter is questioned by the text. Did she laugh because she doubted that God would bring this to pass? At the questioning her laughter stops and she returns to her silence.

Perhaps Sarah did laugh because she doubted it would come to pass. Many of us would have doubts in her position. She had heard promises made before, and the years had widdled away at their seeming truth. Sarah may have laughed because she wasn't sure it would happen this time either, it just seemed so absurd. How could she become pregnant at this age? Or maybe it was because the current circumstances were all just so inexplicable that instead of trying to understand them she decided to simply live in them, throw back her head, and laugh.

One afternoon I sat with a young adult and her mother in a hospital room. Her mother had come in for treatment, and it had been a long evening of emergency testing and waiting for results. The pain came and went, and the teen sat dutifully at her mother's side, offering help as she could. This was not their first visit to emergency care that month, and you could see the strain taking its toll on them both. I entered with what I hoped was a pastoral presence, and listened as they shared about the diagnosis information they had received so far. The hour was growing late, and there was still not a hope of discharge until more tests were returned. Our voices were hushed and the dark circles were beginning to form under their eyes. There were so many questions. The cause of the pain was unknown. Lots of medical information had been shared, but most of it was lost on the exhaustion of the room. None of us understood why this family seemed to have so much pain. They had experienced way more than their share of hospital trips and late nights. Somewhere in the midst of the conversation something struck all three of us as so absurd we started to snicker. Soon the snickering turned in to giggling and the giggles in to fits of laughter. Within a few minutes we were laughing so hard that the nurse stopped in to make sure we were okay (or perhaps that we hadn't all gotten in to the pain medication cabinet when she was away). The laughter brought tears to our eyes and we doubled over in our chairs. It was ridiculous. We were in an emergency room and none of us understood why they were here, again. This was a place full of pain and questions and longing and misunderstanding. And now it was a place where we laughed.

Your life doesn't always make sense. You look at the path you are on and may have plenty of questions for God. You may wonder why you are currently in this place. You may doubt that God is truly at work. You may not understand why things have unfolded the way they have this year. None of us truly understand how God decides when to intervene. Sometimes we get a glimpse. We can put pieces together and see, just for a moment, how God's hand has been moving in the world and in our lives. Events become not just isolated anecdotes but a sequence of stories woven together in a beautiful way we could not have predicted. But these glimpses in to the actions of God are often short and separated by long periods of living one day at a time. We can fight the chaos of our lives, trying to make sense of what is happening around us. We can look for reasons, for cause and effect, for providence. And this is a spiritual process, looking for the divine. Despite our lack of understanding, God is there. When we just want to throw our hands in the air and give up, when the darkness of the chaos of our lives threatens to overwhelm us, we can become obsessed with our need for answers. If you have reached this point, perhaps it is time to stop in the middle of the swirling events of your life. What if you stopped trying to make sense of what is happening, just for a moment, and saw the beautiful chaos that is our lives? What if, just for a moment, you stood with Sarah, at the brink of doubt and despair and confusion, and did the unthinkable. What if you stopped, just for a moment, and laughed?

Chapter 14
INFLUENCE OVER FAME
Side Bars

Several years ago I got a letter in the mail. As I flipped it over and read the return address I groaned loudly. It was from the local courts which could only mean one thing. Jury duty. It was not that I didn't believe in public service. I was grateful to those who served on juries to offer a fair trial of one's peers. But it was one of those weeks that was already overflowing with appointments. My co-worker was out sick. Another was on vacation, which meant my work calendar was full. It was also the week of Halloween. This meant I would have to make good on my commitments made months before as I happily looked through homemade treat and costume ideas. In the next forty eight hours I needed to make twenty four eye ball cupcakes, two batches of snicker doodles and figure out how to make a star wars costume out of cardboard, fabric and glitter paint.

Jury duty waits for no one. But I was optimistic. My friends in ministry had told me that they never select pastors to sit on juries. I brought a few things to read and headed to the courthouse for jury selection. The first hour brought nothing of interest, just checking in of jurors and lawyers. The judge entered, and the work of jury selection began. One at a time they would call our names and we would stand in the jury box to be questioned by the lawyers from the respective sides of the case. One juror would be dismissed, another seated in the jury box. Finally, my name was called.

"Ms. Collins?"
"Yes." I stood.
"Is it correct that you are currently working as a pastor?"
"Yes it is." I smiled and began stacking my papers to put in to my bag.
"And that you are an ordained minister in the Presbyterian church?"
"That's correct!" I began organizing the rest of the day in my mind. If I left soon I could get to both of my meetings and still have time to start on the cupcakes after dinner.
"Is there anything about your position as a pastor that would make you unable to fulfill your duties as a member of this jury in a fair and impartial way?"

I stood quietly for a moment. I had cupcakes to make. I had meetings to attend. But I was under oath. On a Bible no less.

"No?" I said uncertainly.

"Very good. Please take your seat in the jury box."

The images of cupcakes slipped from my mind as I sat next to another jury member and settled in for what became a few days of deliberation. Some of it was what I had expected. There was evidence and presentations to the jury. Witnesses were escorted in and out of the court room to offer their testimony. But there was one thing I had not seen before. Something called the "side bar." Starting from the beginning of jury selection and popping up throughout the rest of the case were these events happening off to the side. A potential juror would be asked a question, and would request a side bar. They would then approach the bench with the judges and lawyers to answer the question in private. More often than not, whatever happened in that side bar led to their dismissal from jury selection. As the evidence was presented later that day, the lawyers would request side bars with the judge before deciding if certain information could be provided to the jury at all. It seemed on the outside that what was important to the case was happening in the center of the courtroom. As the day progressed it became apparent than an equally important but virtually invisible scenario was unfolding in the side bars next to the judge's bench.

There are lots of stories in the bible that take center stage, many of them about men. Most are amazing men of faith. We read of their stories of following God in to uncharted lands. They risk their lives and their fortunes to do great acts of faith. They lead battles with God's people. They carry the gospel message in to hostile communities. They plant churches around the world with the message of Jesus Christ. These men are admirable pioneers of our faith. There are also men in the Bible that play the villain. They are those who worked against the Israelites, against Jesus, against the disciples and early church leaders. They enslave God's people, disparage Jesus' teachings, even crucify the Son of God.

Then there are a few women scattered in the pages of the Bible. They show up often as wives or daughters, and sometimes as leaders in their own rite. Some of these women are included in the pages of this book, prophetesses, mothers, leaders, judges, brave women who carried the message of Jesus, who anointed his body, who led God's people in to battles and through the wilderness. Sometimes women too show up as hinderances to God's purposes instead of supporters. But if we do a side by side comparison, heroes and heroines, villains and vilenesses, it is hardly an equal number. Even the women who have stories included in the pages of the Bible are not always named.

But they were there. The women of Israel, the women of Jesus' day, the women of the early church, they were there. They were working, they were caring for families, they were contributing to their communities. They too heard the prophesies and promises. They too built the community of God's people and survived its persecution. They were there when Jesus was born. When he was crucified. When he rose. They were there when the church was started and the communities of faith began to grow.

These women do not have their stories recorded in the pages of the Bible. They are not studied in Bible courses. There are not children named after them generations after their death by faithful families. They are the invisible characters in the Biblical drama, essential to its unfolding but unknown to the people. They are not women of fame. They are women of influence. They weren't at the center of the biblical drama, but they influenced it just as much. They were living in the side bars.

Perhaps some of us may go on to have our names written in history books. Some women today will go on to be presidents, famous doctors, writers or actresses. With persistence, hard work, and often a stroke of good luck, fame becomes reality. These women will be remembered for generations after their lives by name, celebrated for their public contributions to society. In this generation there is little women cannot do, and the glass ceiling continues to rise higher. We are grateful to these women for their talents and persistence, and they give us hope for what is possible. We pray for these women that God will use them to influence the people in positive ways. Maybe you are in a position of substantial fame and power. Maybe you stand at the center of the courtroom. As you reflect on where God has placed you, how can you be a part of the movement of God's spirit in your community? How can you use the position you have to bring justice to a broken world? How can you be a public voice for creating good around you?

But what about the rest of us? What about those of us whose lives seem ordinary? Do our lives count if after we live and die the only ones who remember us are our close family and friends? What if we feel invisible? If we do not achieve fame and a public legacy, what are our lives really worth?

Everything. The unnamed, unmentioned women of the Bible were a vital piece of the story of God. God was working through their gifts and courageous spirits. It wasn't their fame that affected the community. It wasn't their enduring story. It was their influence.

It is easy to look at the lives of those who are famous and dream of being in that kind of position. But you have been given gifts and abilities to serve God. As you look at your life, you have opportunities that are unique to your time and situation. The women in the headlines, despite their fame, do not personally know the people you know. They do not work where you work, shop where you shop, eat dinner with the people around your table. They were not born with the specific gifts you have in your life. You may not be famous. But you are a woman of influence.

When I was a teenager I had darkened the door of the church maybe a handful of times. My faith experiences were predominately centered around the big holidays, and I don't believe I could have pointed Jesus out in a lineup. Religion was not a central force in my life, but was more something on the peripheral. It wasn't that I didn't have access to religion. There were plenty of churches in my town, including a few with big name famous preachers who attracted thousands to their sanctuaries each week. These famous preachers had written books, spoken on television, and one had even served as a religious advisor to the president of the United States. But they weren't a part of my world. After hearing a fear campaign of a local Christian group that had me convinced I was going to be eaten by a overblown dragon scorpion hybrid at the end of days I began to wonder if perhaps I hadn't given enough thought to what I believed. I began to read through some of the pages of a Bible, but felt lost as to where to begin. Then I met Christa. Christa was a young woman in my class, and she ran the Christian club that met after school. She was shy and unassuming but friendly and encouraged me to come. Christa was not famous by anyone's standards. She was not even popular in our grade. But over the course of that year her leadership in the club at school gave feet to the faith that would sustain me since. Christa wasn't famous. She won't be in any history books. But she chose to be a woman of influence in my life.

What would your life look like if you chose to embrace the influence you have on those around you? How would you live differently if you realized that your actions and words mattered in the building of God's communities around the world? How would it effect your sense of purpose if you saw yourself as an essential piece to the works of justice in the community?

Ending Thoughts
CHOOSE THIS DAY
Life behind Bars

The church I served decided to explore volunteering in our local women's prison. Working with inmates is always something I had wanted to try, but I had never had the opportunity. Or perhaps I had been more hesitant than I realized. My friend Kristin and I agreed to go together to meet with a staff member there, joined by another congregation member who had volunteered previously in the facility. The week leading up to our meeting, anxiety about the trip came out through our laughter. We would wait for someone to ask where we were going on Friday so we could respond "We are going to prison!" We checked in at the prison on Facebook, and we joked about prison selfies and hashtags. The jokes continued on the ride out to the facility, and in to the front doors. Our levity carried us through the initial security checks and sign in procedures. With the unmistakable click of the barred doors locking behind us, our anxious giggles finally subsided. We were now in the locked facility. I am not sure what I expected. The women there were just .... women. Outside of their uniforms, there was nothing about them that looked any different than Kristin or I. Some were young, some were older. One had made a birthday cake for a fellow inmate using only a microwave. Some smiled and greeted us as we walked. I felt my anxiety decreasing and my heart clench as I realized how many preconceived notions I must have had about what the people would look like on the other side of the barbed wire I had driven past so many times before.

A few weeks later I returned to the facility with Kristin and another volunteer Errik to receive our final training. This time I felt much more comfortable with the routine. I made sure there was nothing in my pockets to set off the metal detectors. I had my driver's license ready for the guard at check in. I only jumped slightly when the door locked behind us and we entered the secured part of the prison. I felt a new confidence in this once unfamiliar place, and entered in to the volunteer orientation room with ease.

The staff member welcomed us and handed out large packets of paper. We were told each contained more forms to be filled out, along with the results of our background checks. Having had these done numerous times for work, I casually flipped to my background screening results, giving it a glance and knowing it would be clear.

My eyes perused the papers and paused briefly when I noticed a highlighted sentence under the screening results. I glanced over at Kristin's paperwork, thinking this must be an example of what a criminal record would look like. When I didn't see anything on her front page, I leaned over and whispered, "Yours has this too, right? It's an example?" She glanced over at my paper, looked at me with a grin and replied "nope." My heart skipped a beat and I leaned the other direction to look at Errik's report. "Your paperwork has this highlighted sentence, right?" He looked over at my paper and chucked, "Nope - just yours!" The hand holding my background check report shook, and my other hand shot in to the air. "Excuse me," I called to the staff member. "There has been a mistake on my background check. I know mine is clear." Without looking up she asked, "What does it say?" Trying to keep my voice calm, I replied "It says I have charges that I know are false." "What are they for?" I took a deep breath. "Prostitution and Failing to Appear." Without a second look she gestured in the direction of a very well armed muscular guard. "Our investigator does the background checks. Talk to him."

Admittedly at this point my imagination had run out of control. I knew the report was a mistake. I knew my background check was clear. I also knew that I was sitting on the inside of the barbed wire of a women's prison, and that they believed I not only had a record for prostitution, but that I had never shown up for my court date. The logical part of my brain assured me that it would all be worked out. My paranoid subconscious was already drafting my first letter to my children from behind bars. Next to me my friend made a comment about perhaps someone had misunderstood what the offering plate really was for. I shot him a withering glance and stood up.

I walked quickly over to the investigator and explained that there must be some mistake. He looked at the charges listed on my report, looked at me, and said a skeptical "Okay." I grew insistent. "No! It's a mistake! I'm a *pastor*" putting extra stress on my job title. He shrugged and said "They run it by your social security number. I can run it again, I guess?" "Let's do that!" I said quickly, and returned to my seat, my heart pounding in my ears.

I tried to focus on the training video, but my eyes kept glancing toward the door where the investigator had left, holding my report. Thirty minutes later the phone in the training room rang, and the staff member went to take the call. She looked in my direction and called "Ms. Collins? A call for you." At this my mind flooded with a thousand scenarios of what might happen next. This was how my autobiography of "life behind bars" would start. Someone had stolen my identity, I would have to serve time for a crime I didn't commit.

I would lose my job, and maybe my family. I would have to trade in my volunteer badge for an inmate badge, my Sperry shoes for an orange jumpsuit. As I stood to walk to the phone, I accidentally said a four letter word in my distress. The other good hearted volunteers around me, who are arguably better Christians, looked somewhat scandalized that not only was this pastor a prostitute, but she also had a mouth like a sailor.

I picked up the phone, trying not to panic, or rather trying not to let my panic show. "Ms. Collins?" the low voice of the investigator rumbled on the other end of the line. "Yes?" I squeaked in return. His voice became lighter. "I accidentally put in the number of another person's file instead of yours. Your background check came back clear. Will you still pray for me?"

In those tense moments inside the barbed wire fence, I had a deep clarity of what was really important to me. I was no longer concerned with what time my next meeting would be that day. It didn't matter that there was a sink full of dishes still soaking in my sink from dinner the night before. What I did think about was my family and how much my time with them was worth. I thought about my life and what I still wanted had left to do. I thought also about my crazy faith in an unpredictable and yet reliable God who had brought me to that place.

Our lives are busy. Days blur in to weeks and into years. Children grow up. Jobs change. Health is fleeting. Relationships develop. Through all of these transitions, one thing remains constant. God. Our faith certainly waxes and wanes. We will have days where we feel close to God and can even hear the voice of the Holy Spirit whispering to us. In those moments faith seems a given, not to be questioned. There are also those periods of time where God seems far away. Doubt seeps in, or even more insidious, apathy. We strain to see a Holy God in the middle of our daily lives and come up short. We become so preoccupied with the demands of life that faith becomes at best an afterthought.

In the business of our lives, in the ups and downs of our faith, we are faced with constant choices. We decide what we will eat for breakfast, what we will wear to the gathering that evening, what we want to study. These choices command our attention and seem to be the business of the day. Less obvious but arguably more important are the choices we have considered together in these pages. Will we chose love, honesty and courage? Will we chose to set aside our to-do lists to attend to the people around us? Will we chose to remember what really matters, as we see them in those briefly afforded moments of clarity? Will we chose to respond to the unconditional, life changing love of God?

Years ago a woman led a prayer meditation for a group I was in. She used as a basis Psalm 46 which says, "Be still and know that I am God." Then she repeated the phrase, taking off a word from the end each time, until the final prayer was simply "be." I loved the quiet meditation of the prayer, and appreciated the emphasis it put on each word. With the removal of one word, the phrase took on a completely different meaning for me.

The core of this book is based on choice. The first verse that comes to many of us when we think about choice is from Joshua 24:14 "Choose this day whom you will serve (as for me and my household we will serve the lord)." (NRSV) What if we followed the same pattern of prayer, using this verse as our guide?

Choose this day whom you will serve.
  Who will you serve today? Schedules? Money? Plans? Perfection? When you think through your day, how can you refocus on God so that these things come second? How does how you spend your time, energy and money today reflect where you have placed your priorities?

Choose this day whom you will.
  You have choices, and they are yours alone to make. When we don't consciously chose to decide, the choices are made for us. Each of us experience an unexplainable freedom as children of God. God could accomplish any of God's purposes without us. Or with a fleet of well trained robots. But instead God has chosen humans, with their mistakes and frailties, to be a part of this great work. You have a choice to be a part of this, but it is a choice. Even though God's love is so great we can not possibly resist it, we still, one decision at a time, can make choices to go our own way.

Choose this day whom you.
  Who will you chose to be today? As you fill your role as friend, parent, co-worker, spouse, child, how will you live in to those roles as a disciple of Christ? Will you be able to keep in mind your purpose as you move throughout your day, using your gifts and abilities to highlight the grace of God? As you make these choices, how will they effect who are you in the years to come?

Choose this day who

Who might be a person that needs your time today, who may ask you to set aside the to-do list and walk with them? Who could you offer special attention to as you go through your schedule? Is there someone who has been on your heart to approach for reconciliation, or to offer a word of support?

Choose this day

This day is all we have. Yesterday is over and tomorrow is never promised. What can you do to let go of the past and live fully in the present? Are you living the reality before you or are you holding off for an imagined perfection tomorrow? What reminders can you put throughout your day to stay grounded in the present?

Choose this

Even when we chose this day, we find ourselves missing out on the moments. Is there a way you can try to chose the person or the situation right in front of you, right now, even if it makes you uncomfortable or challenges you in some way?

Choose.

The choice is yours. You can choose Reality. Love. Hope. Courage. Growth. People. Wisdom. Honesty. Openness. Reconciliation. Laughter. Influence. Present. Purpose.

God.

About the Author

Megan Collins lives in Ohio with her husband and two sons.
She is a writer, a public speaker and a Presbyterian pastor.

She dedicates this book to Dave, Mac and Andrew, and the others in her life
who bring laughter to the everyday and show her a glimpse of our great God.